The Battle of New Orleans

An Informal History of the War
That Nobody Wanted: 1812

The Battle of New Orleans

An Informal History of the War That Nobody Wanted: 1812

By DONALD BARR CHIDSEY

CROWN PUBLISHERS, INC. NEW YORK

Contents

Contents

Chapter 1

THERE WAS NO sign of life around Negril Bay at the western tip of Jamaica on a late October morning of the year 1814 when H.M.S. *Pigmy* put in.

No gulls flew. No smoke stood against the sky. Nothing stirred on the blank, light-colored hills or in the swamp that stippled the shore between North Negril and South Negril points. There were no walls or fields, no pasture, in the hinterland, only an occasional gawky oldmaidish coconut tree or a clump of scrub palmetto that shimmered in the light of the sun. True, there were a few scattered huts, dumpy, dun, drab, made of thatch and looking for all the world like haystacks; but either these were mere way stations, overnight stops for far-ranging cattlemen, or food magazines, or else, if they were ordinarily inhabited, the inhabitants now were crouching in fear or had fled—perhaps to the swamp?—at sight of *Pigmy*.

The swamp itself had a sinister aspect. It was not deep, but it was dark. Made up of mangroves, moss-hung trees that crooked and hooked knobby kneelike roots into the edge of the sea, it might have been some monstrous saurian, a gigantic alligator that watched without blink the approach of the war vessel. No sound came from it. Conceivably men, of a sort, were hidden there. The swamp may have masked a smattering of maroons, escaped slaves who had gone wild, who spoke no known language and wore no clothes, who killed animals and men alike with their bare hands, for they had no weapons. The maroons [1] were not often seen, for they were as shy as fairies, as elusive as mist; but they could make themselves felt; and when they did strike, they left nothing.

Pigmy was just that, as war vessels went—a pigmy. Schooner-

1

rigged, small, low, fast, she carried only six guns, clearly a dispatch runner, a scout.

If the men aboard this vessel had heard of the maroons—as seems almost certain—they showed no fear. Within ten minutes of the time the anchor had been let go, startlingly close inshore, every boat the schooner carried was being put overside—longboat, moses, even the gig. Soon a score of men were poking into as many parts of the swamp, sampling pools of water, testing the flow, blazing trees. Were they in seach of deserters? Hardly—in so remote a place. No; any tar, watching, would have known what it was. Not beef, for cattle would have been seen if scattered across those bare slopes; and not fresh fruit, for there would be precious little of that in such a dank hole, and none at all that an honest mariner might trust. Well, what was it that vessels after a long voyage most need when they touch shore? Why, water and firewood.

The men from *Pigmy* were taking very little wood and water —perhaps they had not come far?—but they were marking on maps and in their minds the spots where these could be found. This meant that others were to follow them; these mariners were only preparing the way; *Harbinger* would have been a better name for the craft they had come in.

The war that nobody wanted had been going badly, for both sides. But soon it would be over. A vast armada was about to be assembled here in Negril Bay, a vast army. Great Britain was cocking her fist for the knockout blow.

Chapter 2

IMPRESSMENT NEVER had been authorized by law, but neither did any law forbid it, while various Parliamentary enactments had recognized its existence without expression of disapproval.

The English in particular had a squelching argument in favor of impressment: "Why, that's the way it's always *been!*" This was not strictly true; but beyond doubt the custom was old, being indeed a vestige left over from feudalism. The king, that greatest baron of them all, at any time could command the services of his subjects, whether at labor, in battle, or on the sea. They belonged to him, like his palaces, like his queen. All impressment, no matter how dirty, was done in the name of the crown.

The very name of the practice reflects this, coming as it does not from the English verb *to press,* meaning to crush, to crowd, or flatten, but rather from the medieval French adjective *prest* (now *prêt*), meaning ready. This too could become a verb: to prest a man was to make him ready for service by means of the prest, or gift money, or bounty, which in Great Britain always was called the king's shilling, a coin that held a profound mystical meaning and legally carried all the strength of a signature.

Toward the end of the eighteenth century and in the beginning of the nineteenth impressment was associated with the navy. There were sundry reasons for this. The navy, which once had been no more than an emergency organization, a set of armed merchant ships recruited for a special occasion, recently had become a full-time specialized professional service, and more recently still, because of the all but continuous war with France—it had broken out again in 1793, and though peace was declared in 1802 it was an uneasy peace and everybody knew that it would soon be broken—as it was, a year later. Meanwhile a disagreeable small meteor by the name of Napoleon Bonaparte had started to streak across the European sky, and it was clear at once that you couldn't do business with such a person, who was no gentleman, being all guile, an utterly unpredictable liar: this would be a fight to the death. So the British Navy had been enormously enlarged. It was made up of hundreds of vessels, thousands of mariners: there was a man in the Royal Navy for every two hundred men, women, and children in the British Isles; and since Trafalgar, fought in 1805, it had been far-and-away the largest navy in the world, indeed the only mentionable one. It must stay that way. The very life of the islands it guarded hung upon this superiority, as everybody knew.

The army seldom needed recourse to the press gang. It didn't often have to hit men on the head and slip the king's shilling into their pockets before they could recover, though this had been done. The army had three reservoirs of cannon fodder—Ireland, the Scottish highlands, and public jails all over the kingdom. For almost any man could be made a soldier, somehow. A soldier was not called upon to think; and in fact, it was better for all concerned if he didn't. He was not required to aim his musket, only hold it in a prescribed position and fire at command. A soldier might die, but that too should be only at command.

With the seaman or mariner—they resented being called sailors, God knows why—it was different. Not only must he be tough, even tougher than the soldier if he was to survive for long the appalling conditions aboard warships, the brutal discipline, the rotten food, the backbreaking work, but he must also have skill. Though kicked around, he was in his way an artisan. It wasn't easy to replace him.[2]

It was, however, easy to *spot* him. His profession stuck out all over the wretch—in his walk and his talk, in the tar that clung to him, the slop-chest clothes he wore, the oaths he swore. He drank and stank like a seaman. He even sang sea songs, chanteys (which he pronounced *sh*anties). It was said of the seaman that if he went more than a mile from the waterfront he couldn't even get his hair cut without the aid of an interpreter. This, together with his habit of drinking himself blind as quickly as possible, made him easy to recover.

Not that the Royal Navy cared for the man himself. It was the principle of the thing. It was the example. In any event, the poor devil was of little further use to the Royal Navy *as a hand*. If he wasn't hanged—hanging was the legal punishment for desertion but it was not always inflicted, the cat-o'-nine-tails being thought a more impressive exhibition—he was given so savage a beating at the gangway (or series of beatings, for it was entirely up to the captain and there are cases on record of as many as seven hundred lashes being laid on one bare back, a process that took some weeks, since there would be no sense lashing a man who had fainted from pain) that he was a gibbering idiot for the rest of his life.

But what could he do? When he awoke after his spree, and found that his pockets had been picked, even if he escaped the press gang or the crimps who would have returned him for punishment, which way should he turn? He was fit only for the sea. That was the life he knew. Anything else would have confused him.

The story of the sailor who after being paid off put an oar over his shoulder and started to walk inland with the announcement that he planned to settle down in the first place where somebody asked him what that thing was, is at least as old as Homer; but there could hardly have been many such among the deserters from the British Navy.

The logical place for our deserter was another vessel, preferably an American one.

There were two reasons for this. The common language was one: even English and American landsmen talked much the same, and the lingo of the mariners was identical. The other reason was the treatment and the pay on American vessels. They, too, badly needed men, for in a world rent with war the chief neutral was catching an expanded carrying trade; and they were willing to pay, even, in some cases, to the extent of supplying a man with one of those "protections" intended to prove that he was American-born and so not subject to impressment.

There were two kinds of "protections"—general protections issued to skippers and covering their whole crews, and certificates of protection issued by consuls or by justices of the peace or notaries public to individual seamen, each of whom thereupon was declared to be of American birth. In the early days the United States had asked only that a reputable person had lived within its limits one year, after which time he could become a citizen, though by the Constitution he was never able to be President. Lately this was fourteen years, which might have been supposed to satisfy anybody. It didn't satisfy Great Britain.

Perhaps some of the general protections and surely many of the individual protections were fakes. The British believed or pretended to believe that they all were, and not infrequently they ripped these papers to shreds before the eyes of the man they were impressing; for this entire business was made even more unpleasant by the fact that hauteur had become a required attitude in the British Navy, a service in which courtesy was held in contempt, while an officer's arrogance was as much a part of his equipment as was his sword.

That is, the British Navy ruled the world; and it wished to make sure that everybody understood this.

By law all who held commissions in this navy were gentlemen, and in truth, at home, some were; but the rigid requirements of sea duty called for the quashing of every trace of good manners when there was any contact with a "foreigner," so that the midshipmen and lieutenants at least (captains were exalted enough to permit their natural feelings to show) were insufferable.

"Keep the pay, keep the man," was a saying believed in by many R.N. captains, though times without number it had been proved to be false. On one excuse or another, sometimes with no excuse at all, the pay, pitifully small at best, was docked or was withheld. Even so, only a few of the most trusted seamen, in particular those who worked in press gangs, ever were allowed ashore; and the average mariner would spend months and even years at a time without setting foot on land.

Not for humanitarian reasons but in an effort to plug the leak of desertion, there were certain somewhat ameliorating practices.

The hold and the orlop, the unspeakable nether regions, where fresh air never was permitted to penetrate, were periodically fumigated by the burning of brimstone soaked in vinegar, a combination that didn't cause them to be any the less malodorous but did keep down, a little, the bugs.

There was the grog issue, half a gill a day, which, if saved, and if the saved portion wasn't stolen—a stabbing offense—could in time be induced to numb any man for a few hours.

Finally, and though much of the patrol work had to be done in the West Indies or in the Mediterranean, or off the coast of France, or, once this new war was started on the side, the coast of America, nevertheless there were times when the warship had to put into a British port for restocking or refitting; and on such occasions, which might last a month or more, the benign or cautious captain, though he wouldn't dream of granting any shore leave, usually did permit the men to have their wives or sweethearts aboard. Temporary households thus were set up; and since any kind of privacy was hard to come by aboard a ship of the line, connubial or extralegal bliss had to be snatched wherever a chance offered, beneath one of the cannons being the best place—hence the expression "son of a gun."

For all of this, the ungrateful salts slipped ashore whenever they could; and many of them, perhaps most, lying about their origin, signed on board of American vessels, whether merchantman or warship.

As long as the press gangs stayed ashore, napping befuddled seamen in the rum shops of London, Bristol, Liverpool, Kingston, Nassau, Gibraltar, the United States, though many of these men claimed to be American, could do little but protest and through specially appointed agents try to obtain their release, a complex and uncertain process. But when in 1796 the British began to stop vessels willy-nilly on the high seas and search them for any able-bodied man the boarding officer cared to call a deserter from the British Navy, then Washington began a series of very loud, persistent squawks.

The British did more. Though war with America was hardly even talked of at the time, they sent over frigates that hovered outside the principal American ports, just a few miles offshore, and with shots-across-the-bow commanded incoming and outgoing vessels to stand and be searched. One of those shots, too close, outside New York harbor killed an innocent American, which of course made for a great deal of hard feeling.

A well-developed, firm, staunch nation would have resented

such treatment; but Great Britain, like France, assumed that this new little republic would bob its head in obedience.

Even those British deserters who joined the United States Navy learned that they were not safe, as they'd supposed. Four such, men who had lately slipped over the side of *Melampus,* one of the warships watching Norfolk, Virginia, enlisted in the United States Navy at Norfolk, where the brand-new frigate, *Chesapeake,* fresh from the navy yard at Washington and thanks to departmental inefficiency already late for her assignment in the Mediterranean, had stopped to complete her crew. The four made no bones about their desertion, but insisted that they had only been in the British Navy in the first place because, though Americans, they'd been impressed. They said they were all American born. Three in fact were. The fourth, a man named Ratford—though he'd enlisted in the United States Navy as "Wilson"—lied. Captain Gordon questioned all four personally, and believed them. When the British admiral, Berkeley, sent in to demand their return, this was refused.

June 21, 1807, *Chesapeake* sailed out. Just beyond the three-mile limit she was hailed by *Leopard,* one of the British frigates, which sent an officer aboard of *Chesapeake.* This officer demanded that he be allowed to muster the *Chesapeake's* crew and pick out the four deserters. Commodore James Barron, Gordon's superior, replied that this was against U.S. Navy regulations. They bowed to one another, and the British officer went back to *Leopard,* which immediately afterward opened fire.

It was unbelievable, but it happened. Barron was helpless. Because of the delay in Washington—not his fault—he had planned to mount his guns at sea, to save time. He didn't have so much as a bow-chaser in firing position when *Leopard* opened up. After all, why should he? The United States was not at war, and pirates were not to be expected a few miles off Norfolk, Virginia. Match tubs, swabbers, scrapers, rammers, sponges, linstocks, wormers—all were stored below, together with the very powder and ball.

The bombardment continued for fifteen minutes, at a pistol shot's length, badly damaging *Chesapeake.* Barron did manage to get one gun mounted and loaded, and he fired a single token shot—an officer ran all the way from the galley with a live coal in his hand to do this—and then he struck.

He had to. Three of his men were dead. Eighteen others, including himself, were wounded. The deck was a shambles.

The British officer came back, bowed, refused to accept the surrender of the ship (for, he explained, the two nations were not at war) and mustered the American crew on deck and picked out and took away his four deserters.

Chesapeake limped back to Norfolk. *Leopard* went to Halifax, where Ratford-Wilson was hanged. One of the other kidnapped men died in the British service the following year, in the West Indies. The other two were ceremoniously returned to the deck of *Chesapeake,* with apologies, two years later. Great Britain also agreed to pay reparations to the wounded and to the families of the dead. But by that time the damage had been done. Nor was Admiral Berkeley (though Barron was suspended without pay for five years) ever punished.

Thomas Jefferson had all he could do to keep his country quiet after this insult, and his prayer throughout those last months of his second and final term was that he would not have to sign a declaration of war. He succeeded, just; and on March 4, 1809, he turned over the Presidency to his fellow Virginian, James Madison.

Madison was "a plain and rather mean-looking little man, of great simplicity of manners." He walked with a bouncy step, had receding hair, preferred black clothes, and didn't care for these new-fashioned double-breasted coats. He suffered from bilious attacks. Sometimes called "the non-oratorical Virginian," he never raised his voice, never laughed aloud, and said what little he had to say as though he had just at that instant thought of it. It was impossible to guess what he was thinking, though surely he was. Everybody knew, however, that he was a Jeffersonian, an "old Republican," [3] and a man of peace. When he ceased to be Secretary of State and became President there would be no wrenching change in administration.

Some Congressmen there were, who, like some editors,

clamored for prompt and violent action. Wright of Maryland, for instance, introduced a bill into the House classifying impressment on the high seas as piracy and calling for the death penalty, by means of two-hundred-dollar prizes encouraging mariners to resist the press gang anywhere and in any form, absolving them of blame if they killed or hurt any member of such a gang, and providing that their pay should continue and be held for them at home all the time they were forced to serve in the British Navy, the funds for this being taken from seized British property in the United States. This would have been a declaration of war, and the country wasn't ready for it, or at any rate Congress wasn't; so the Wright bill was kicked into some corner of a committee room, where it was allowed to die.

There were zealous, honest, earnest efforts to settle the dispute, especially, understandably, on the part of the Americans. The United States ambassadors to Great Britain at this time, Pinkney, Rufus King, Monroe, were exceptionally able men; and if the same could not be said of the British ambassadors to Washington this was because Great Britain had much more important matters on her mind and didn't believe that her former colonies could be forced into a fight anyway, since they had nothing to fight *with*.

Twice the dove of peace fluttered anxiously overhead, looking for a place to land.

One of the British ambassadors, a favorite in this country, Erskine, exceeded his authority when he made an informal agreement with the State Department that looked for a little while like a full settlement: he was immediately recalled and reprimanded, and the whole thing fell through.

A little before that, Monroe and Pinkney, struggling in London, for a moment ignored *their* orders that there must be no treaty that did not specifically disavow the theory and practice of impressment. They agreed to a treaty without any mention of impressment, obtaining at the same time a solemn note of assurance that the practice would be supervised and that all American protests would receive immediate and scrupulous attention—much more than Britain until that time had conceded and more than she was likely to concede in the future. As Pinkney and Monroe explained when they forwarded this note to Washington, along with the treaty, because of British public opinion the Foreign Office at Whitehall simply could not risk a disavowal of the practice of impressment, but informally and unofficially this amounted to the same thing. Jefferson, still President, didn't agree. For all his love of peace, he refused even to submit this treaty to the Senate.

Thereafter the Foreign Office attitude, like that of the British admiralty, stiffened, showing much shortness of temper. "We haven't got time for such quibbling," England seemed to say. "We're wrestling with the worst threat to human liberty ever to appear on the historical horizon, and we're doing this alone, mind you. So keep quiet, you over there." To which, from time to time, Britain might have added: "And if you think *we're* high-handed, you with all your talk of freedom, how would you like to have *Boney* calling the turn?"

The marrow of the matter seldom was approached. This was the doctrine of indefeasible (or indelible) allegiance, subscribed to by virtually every country in the world excepting that brash new little one in North America, which was putting forward the doctrine of voluntary expatriation.

England and the others believed that what you were born you remained, and that you could no more change your nationality than you could change your skin: this had nothing to do with law, for it was self-evident. The United States, on the other hand, a nation made up of outsiders in the first place, contended that a sovereign state could accept—on her own terms, to be sure—the allegiance of anybody who cared to offer it.

That's what it boiled down to, and the question never was settled.

In the course of the many negotiations on impressment— there were twelve separate ones, over a period of twenty years —more than one American diplomat pointed out that Great Britain extended British citizenship to foreigners who had served in British ships during a period of war for two years, though such citizens, or subjects, would not be permitted to serve in Parliament or hold any civil or military position or receive any royal grant of land. In other words, England was claiming for herself a right she denied to every other nation when she made the pronouncement: "Once an Englishman always an Englishman." The Foreign Office never stooped to answer this. Great Britain could afford to be inconsistent. She was strong enough.

So it went, getting steadily worse. While Madison was Secretary of State, from 1801 to 1809, he forwarded more than 2,000 cases of alleged impressed American seamen to London, and fewer than 200 of these were in time freed. When hostilities at last broke out, in June of 1812, there were on record in Washington more than 6,000 registered cases of illegal impressment. If these were all honest—admittedly a large assumption—it meant that there were more American seamen in the British Navy than there were in the navy of the United States. Which was an odd way to start a war.

Chapter 3

Pigmy NO LONGER was alone at Negril Bay. The first of November General Brooke and Admiral Malcolm had arrived with no fewer than 3,500 men, the vanguard.

They were flushed with easy victory, these veterans, and loafing off the western tip of Jamaica was no more than a rest for them, a vacation, while they looked forward to the last fight of the war, which probably wouldn't prove to be a fight at all but just another chase.

The bay was crisscrossed at all daylight hours by brightly polished gigs, for there was a great deal of visiting among the officers. There were cards, and some dice. There were cockfights too, and dogfights, even a few pugilistic exhibitions. It was all very gay, very jolly.

The maroons, if there really were any of them watching from their secret places, must have marveled to learn that there were so many men on earth, and must have wondered what they were here for. If so, the maroons were alone. The rest of the world knew.

New Orleans, that lush, lovely, soggy, sweet city, was a plum for the picking, and had been so since the outbreak of war two and a half years ago. New Orleans, bless her heart, was rich, dissatisfied, and virtually helpless.

"The City of New Orleans is not Fortified, nor furnished with the means either for Hostile or Defensive operations," James Lucas Yeo, then a captain in the British Navy, now Sir James and an admiral in charge of the Great Lakes, had reported the previous year.

"Almost the whole of their Troops (consisting of undisciplined Militia) have been sent to Mobile for the purpose of seizing on Pensacola and every other part of the Spanish Possessions in West Florida. . . .

"The Banks of the River are composed of soft mud, and the Town, which is embanked to protect it from inundation, is consequently ill calculated for Bombardment. . . ." [4]

French-speaking Louisiana had been given nothing to say about her sale to the United States, which jolted her, and she didn't know whether she liked it. She had little enough to do with the rest of the country, and only a few weeks before the declaration of war had she herself been admitted as a state; she had not been represented in Congress at the time of that vote. Certainly she didn't think much of the federal army, from what she had seen of it, and with reason. First there was General James Wilkinson, an almost incredibly corrupt man, bombastic to boot. Wilkinson had been succeeded by Brigadier General Flournoy, who, if he wasn't as objectionable as his predecessor, didn't seem to take much interest in his job, and who in July of this year 1814 quit without notice, to go home, leaving New Orleans (and it hurt her pride) commanded only by a colonel.

The lately appointed commanding officer of this federal military district, a major general named Jackson, never had been seen in New Orleans, a place he seemed to be trying to avoid, though repeatedly asked to go there; for he was obsessed with the idea that the British would first strike Mobile. Nobody in New Orleans knew much about this man Jackson, but he was a Northerner, and that was enough. (Actually he came from Tennessee, but to those in New Orleans anybody from that far up the river was a barbarous Kaintuk, or Kentuckian, when he wasn't a Yanqui, or Yankee.)

Only New England, until lately, had escaped the blockade the British had fastened on the American coast early in the war: New England had been spared, at first, because the cunning English knew from their spies that New England was a hotbed of dissension and if treated right might break away from the Union and make a separate peace. There was a certain amount of smuggling into and out of New Orleans, of course; there always had been; but it had been impossible, these past two and a half years, to move the heavy stuff, and the warehouses of the city were crammed with cotton and sugar reported to be worth $17,500,000, also tobacco, hemp, and lead, which, together with the shipping stranded there, was worth some $2,500,000 more. Assuredly here was a prize.

But the greatest attraction, at least for the men on top, was New Orleans' position. She controlled the mouth of the Mississippi, which meant, in effect, that she controlled that whole vast rich expanse between the Alleghenies and the Rockies. Without the Mississippi the lusty young republic simply couldn't expand. All those goods in her warehouses, goods so easily converted into cash, would be as nothing to the value of New Orleans as a pawn on the peace table. With this card in her hand Great Britain might bid almost anything.

Captain Henry Percy, R.N., paid a visit to Pensacola, where he left a force of soldiers and marines.

This was, theoretically, Spanish territory; but Spain and England were allies at the moment. The intense desire of President Madison and his Secretary of State, James Monroe, another Virginian, to get the Floridas, was notorious. Already they had grabbed West Florida, including Mobile, on the ground that the Louisiana Purchase had included the Gulf coast as far east as the Sabine River, an argument the Spaniards, being so weak, could do nothing to refute. Pensacola, in East Florida, might be another matter. The Louisiana Purchase could not possibly be stretched *that* far. It was conceivable that this visit of Captain Percy might be used as an excuse by Andrew Jackson to violate the neutrality of the section; but the governor, Don Matteo Gonzales Manrique, wasn't strong enough to shoo them off anyway, so he greeted them with smiles.

Percy dumped Lieutenant Colonel Edward Nicholls, together with a field gun, two howitzers, 100 marines, and 1,000 stand of muskets, on the beach at Pensacola. Then he sailed to Mobile, where he attacked Fort Bowyer, which beat him off, sinking one of his ships.

Meanwhile, Nicholls, an Irishman, evidently picked for this purpose, was talking very big indeed. August 25 he issued a statement urging all inhabitants of this part of the world, assumedly whether in Spanish or U.S. territory, to cast off the yoke of the "faithless, imbecile" government at Washington.

There was nothing extraordinary about this, in itself. Perfervid statements from military personages were the rule. But Nicholls went further. With a handful of men he had under him, and presumably with the thousands of redskins he was about to enlist, he would, he vowed, take New Orleans in a walk. This was ridiculous. Perhaps it was meant to be.

The Indians south of the Ohio were scarcely warlike. There were no Mohawks among them, no Iroquois. Along the east bank of the Mississippi, clear down to the Gulf, the scattered Chickasaws and Choctaws were a mild lot. Alabama, Mississippi, and the western part of Georgia were overrun by the almost equally mild confederacy of Muskogees, or Creeks. Even the eloquent Tecumseh, a latter-day Pontiac, who had visited them from the north recently in an attempt to get them to join his master-confederacy, could not do much to stir spirit in these flabby-spined aborigines. Moreover, they were poorly armed, few having muskets, while none had rifles.

The Alabamas were members of this confederacy, though not Creeks by blood, but they were not numerous. The Seminoles, cousins who some time before had broken from the others to seek out better hunting grounds (the name means "the runaways" or "the wild ones") might be more dangerous. And it was the Seminoles, according to the plan, that Nicholls concentrated upon, teaching them how to use firearms.

Andrew Jackson had no love for the Seminoles, any more than he had for other Indians. "Dependance may be reposed in their fears," he wrote from the field to the Secretary of War, "but not in their friendship." Jackson, who was not above letting off a red-hot proclamation himself, could have told Colonel Nicholls something about the redmen of those parts, as allies. "The inconvenience attending Indians is, that you cannot keep them in the field. As soon as they perform an excursion, and take a scalp, they must go home and have a dance."

This was something that Nicholls still had to learn.

That the British were not choosy with whom they made deals was further proved when on September 3 the brig *Sophie*, R.N., came calling with an offer at Grande Terre, the most notorious den of pirates in the world.

The city of New Orleans is more than a hundred miles from the open Gulf of Mexico, and the intervening country on both sides of the river is treacherous, shifting, squashy, more water than land. It is an aquatic wilderness, made up of quaking prairies, bayous, meandering streams, dead-ended waterways, and cypress swamp. With its pelicans and herons, cranes, flamingos, and kingfishers, with its mallards and pintails and teal, with its 'possum and otter and alligator and bear, with its gar and bream, its black bass, perch, sunnies, and mudfish, it could well have been huzzaed as a sportsman's paradise; but it was no place for an army with an artillery train.

There are five mouths to the Mississippi, and the deepest of these granted only twelve feet at the bar. It was protected by an old fort at Belize, but that could be knocked out, if it was even standing these days. Yet the large vessels, the heaviest laden, the transports, could not get in.

About fifty miles up, at an angle, Fort St. Philip and Fort Bourbon faced one another across the river. Neither amounted to much, according to the British intelligence, and Fort Bourbon when last reported was no more than a ruin; but they might have been rebuilt and rearmed, if this man Jackson knew his business. Farther up still, barely sixteen miles below the city, was the worst place of all, a place called, ironically, English Turn. Here the twist was such that for about three and a half miles the river flowed *north,* and sailing craft—the British had no galleys—even with luck were sure to be held up for at least a few hours, under the guns of a fort that *would* be maintained in good condition, Jackson or no Jackson.

There were other ways of getting there.

East of the mouths of the river a series of small islands hugging the Gulf coast formed a sound that ran all the way to Mobile, and this was an important avenue of coasting trade between the two cities, though the trade was carried on in shallow-draft boats. The western tip of this sound was formed by Lake Borgne, which really was a lagoon, very shallow, opening into a series of bayous and eventually into Lake Ponchartrain, the back door of New Orleans. There were various routes by means of which the city might be approached from Lake Borgne, but all were narrow, and shallow, and while not fortified would be easily defended.

Still closer to the mouths, on the east side, was a route made up of River aux Chiens and the Bayou Terre aux Boeufs, which would lead a man clear up to English Turn, only sixteen miles below the city—but he would have to be a man in a very small boat and he couldn't expect to bring any cannons with him.

West of the mouths there were two principal routes. Bayou La Fourche started at the Gulf about eight miles from the westernmost mouth and extended north right into the Mississippi itself, of which truly it formed a separate mouth. Bayou La Fourche was navigable, but narrow. It could be easily defended.

Barataria Bay, between Bayou La Fourche and the river, had a channel ten feet deep which extended for seventy miles directly north toward New Orleans. After that it was broken into a series of bayous, small streams, and swamps, by means of which, if you had the right guide, you could reach a point on the west bank of the Mississippi right opposite New Orleans. But Barataria was controlled by outlaws.

They were really smugglers, these fabled Baratarians, but the romantic New Orleanaise preferred to think of them as pirates, and indeed there is no doubt that they did indulge in a little piracy now and then. They dealt chiefly in slaves, the importation of whom was forbidden by federal law, but they would also handle wine, brandy, or silks, when these could be made to pay. But slaves, "black ivory," were the most profitable. You put a prime hand down in the barracoons of Grande Terre for perhaps $100, if bargained for at sea, or simply for the expenses of the voyage if you stole him; and he cost little to keep—just easily caught fish; and planters would *come to you* eager to buy him, with gold, at $800.

Nor did slaves take up much room.

The Baratarians operated, outside, under letters of marque authorizing them to prey upon Spanish ships, and issued by the Republic of Cartagena, a new government that nobody, excepting the Baratarians, recognized. Though like most of their kind they were marine scavengers, and would take whatever they could get, they struck usually just north of Cuba on the sea lane that led to Havana, the slave route. They might purchase, at pistol-point, or they might merely take. Then they brought the goods to Grande Terre, the island that guarded the entrance to Barataria Bay, and sold them either to folks in New Orleans or else to plantation owners up and down the river. In this way they did very well for themselves.

Their leader, Jean Lafitte, a smooth, glib, handsome young Gascon-Basque, nominally a New Orleans blacksmith, did not go on these corsairing trips. He wasn't a good sailor: he got sick. But he and his brother, the fat, slow, cross-eyed Pierre, also ostensibly a blacksmith, were exceedingly shrewd businessmen with important commercial and political connections in the city.

The Lafittes had not started this racket, but they took it over and organized it and made it into a big thing. Too big a thing, some thought. It had been going on for too long, and for all its glitter it was getting to be a nuisance, disapproved, if secretly, by the city's more outstanding merchants. The federal government, too, could not be expected to wink forever at a steady smuggling of slaves. No doubt the army and the navy would have descended upon Grande Terre before this if it had not been for the war. Jean Lafitte, who had many spies, knew that the army and navy were thinking of it even then, even as *Sophie,* standing off, sounded her signal gun. Lafitte himself was an outlaw, with a price on his head, and his brother, whom he dearly loved, was a prisoner in the calaboose at New Orleans.

Lafitte had these circumstances in mind when he went out to meet the gig from *Sophie.*

There was a Captain Lockyer, R.N., an unnamed naval lieutenant, and M'Williams, an army captain. All of this Lafitte understood well enough, for his English was good.

Grande Terre, an alp for those parts, was about six miles by three, and the smugglers' colony was largely clustered along the north beach, the inside, on Barataria Bay, leaving the open Gulf side bare; but Jean Lafitte himself had a neat white house in the very center, at the highest point, from the veranda of which, with a glass, he could survey the sea, taking a good peek at each vessel before it got too close. He led his visitors to that house.

There was some jostling on the way, and it might have caused even British officers to quail, at least inwardly, for these Baratarians were ferocious of aspect, true outlaws, the scum of the earth. Lafitte soon settled this, his voice stern, and then he conducted his guests to dinner, which was beyond compare— for the man always lived well, even out there—and plied them with rum and with exquisite, smuggled wine.

(It is possible that the little contretemps on the beach was arranged in advance by Lafitte and was meant to impress the visitors with his authority and control. We will never know).

After the amenities the letters were produced, and Jean Lafitte read them.

There was one from Nicholls, addressed to "Monsieur Lafite, or the Commandant at Barataria," and there was a shrill proclamation, also signed by Nicholls, and addressed, originally, to "Natives of Louisiana!" and later, somewhat confusingly, to "Men of Kentucky!" The proclamation was preposterous, though the letter hinted that it might be well if Lafitte distributed this in New Orleans—where there was a warrant out for his arrest—and the surrounding countryside.

The proclamation boasted of Indian allies and hinted that the slaves might be freed, the worst thing it could possibly have done.

". . . the American usurpation in this country must be abolished . . . you have too long borne grievous impositions. . . ."

The letter was more to the point.

I call on you with your brave followers to enter into the service of Great Britain in which you shall have the rank of Captain: lands will be given to you all in proportion to your respective ranks on a peace taking place. . . . Your ships and vessels to be placed under the orders of the commanding officer of this station. . . . The bearer of this, captain M'Williams will satisfy you on any other points you are anxious to learn. . . . We have a powerful reenforcement on its way here.

The reference to M'Williams suggests that part of the offer was verbal, and popular rumor made this a bribe of $40,000 cash; but it never was anything but rumor.

The two remaining messages were signed by Captain the Hon. William Henry Percy, of H.M.S. *Hermes,* senior officer in the Gulf of Mexico. One, addressed to Lockyer, directed him to make this visit and to offer land and British citizenship to the Baratarians provided they would do as they were told. The other, in veiled terms yet unmistakably, threatened destruction to the settlement unless the Baratarians were co-operative. England, dropping for a moment the doctrine of indelible allegiance, used both carrot and stick.

Jean Lafitte should have been a diplomat. Somehow, by letter to Nicholls but also by word of mouth, he convinced the Britishers that for various reasons he needed a fortnight in which to put his affairs in order, strongly hinting that at the end of that time he and all of his men would be at their service.

Then, as soon as the visitors had gone, Lafitte sat down and wrote to a highly placed friend in New Orleans, sending the proclamation and the letters with this message. He also wrote to the governor of Louisiana, to whom he had asked his friend to show this material. To the governor he suggested a pardon.

He was in a corner and he sought to make a deal. The state people he could still handle, through his connections; it was the federal people he worried about.

He was not to get his deal, yet. The letters caused some talk in high government circles, but a council of war decided against trusting the smuggler, and Commodore D. T. Patterson, ranking U.S. Navy officer in the district, was instructed to go ahead with his preparations for stamping out the colony on Grande Terre.

This Patterson did. The Lafittes—Pierre meanwhile had escaped from the calaboose and rejoined his brother—trailing the stories of buried treasure that are customary on such occasions, went into hiding.

The British would have to find some other route.

These were fleabites. They would make no difference, or little difference, in the invasion. The force at Negril Bay was building up.

Chapter 4

IT WAS A BITTER lesson, but it had to be learned: when most of the world is at war no considerable nation can stay neutral. Previous conflicts had been almost like fist fights, student duels, personal affairs, and the onlooker who was hurt was hurt because he had been stupid enough to get in the way. This was no longer so.

Not only history but geography seemed to be on the American side, so that the noisiest Congressional opponent of war, Randolph of Roanoke, could cry: "We have—thank God!—in the Atlantic a fosse wide enough and deep enough to keep off any immediate danger to our territory." Randolph must have been one of the first to make that mistake. For it was upon the surface of this very "fosse" that most of the trouble occurred; and if in the West the war was to be largely a matter of real estate, in the East it was largely a matter of trade.

The Virginians who were running the country were by no means stupid, and they were passionately devoted to peace, and willing to try, as they did try, economic sanctions in the place of threats; but for all their efforts, persisted in over a long period of time, it became increasingly evident, to them as to everybody else, that sooner or later they would have to take sides. That was the way the world worked.

It was hard to choose, but it had to be done.

The Americans were of Anglo-Saxon stock. The language they spoke, both masses and classes, differed so little from that spoken in England that it could not even be designated as a dialect.[5] Americans read English books, quoted English poets, sang English songs. True, America had fought a long war with Great Britain in order to gain her freedom, and it was true too that without the aid of France she never would have won that war, that freedom. Since then, however, the United States also had fought an undeclared naval war with France. Since then too France had staged her own revolution, a singularly messy one, by which no nation was more shocked than was the young United States. The situation was made even more complicated by the extraordinary repulsiveness, in American eyes, of Napoleon Bonaparte.

He was a monster. Should we pretend that we esteemed him no more than a passing, if horrid, phenomenon? or should we, like Beethoven when he tore up the dedication of his *Eroica Symphony,* admit in public that we had been mistaken?

One thing at least was certain: there was no saying "a plague o' both your houses." Circumstances wouldn't permit this.

Trafalgar should be set down as a date (October 21, 1805) as important in American as in English or French history. Since that battle the whole pattern was changed, on both sides of the sea. If the Corsican no longer could hope to conquer England by invasion—and conquer he must, if he was to go on controlling all of continental Europe—he made plans to do so by means of money, trade. He who had so liked to hear England sneered at as a nation of shopkeepers would, he hoped, bankrupt her. If England couldn't transship, if she could not peddle her wares, he knew, she would have to cry for help; and her principal market was the continent of Europe; so he closed the ports of the continent to her.

Great Britain quite naturally retaliated by blockading France.

That is, they were blockading one another; and the United States, by far the most important neutral, with most of the carrying trade, was caught in between.

The Napoleonic measures were known as the Berlin Decree and the Milan Decree. The British measures were known as orders-in-council. They were both illegal, in American eyes, and on paper equally offensive. In fact, the orders-in-council were the more offensive just because the British *did* command the seas. Though the French fleet was bottled in half a dozen harbors, with watchful British warships standing off and on to be sure that they stayed there, now and then a French frigate did slip loose and cause a lot of damage; and there were also the French privateers, for according to Napoleon's decrees any American ship could be confiscated, along with all its cargo, if it had been so much as searched in passing by a British cruiser; and the British themselves, seemingly, were everywhere.

Neither side was prepared to discuss at any length or with even a show of good temper the timely questions involved—

what was a real blockade as distinguished from a paper block-ade? what constituted contraband? was the doctrine of con-tinuous voyage (a doctrine so complicated that even maritime law experts of the time were not sure what it meant) [6] no longer valid, and if so, why?

It might be supposed that each of the parties at war would make at least a show of conciliation toward the harassed neutral, if only for the purpose of causing her to turn upon the other one. Nothing of the sort happened. They were too busy bat-tling, those giants, to be bothered by the wails of a Johnny-come-lately from across the Atlantic; and indeed they seemed to vie with one another in insulting the United States.[7]

It was more than once proposed that we go to war with France as the safest thing to do. We could then show the world that we were willing to fight, and yet not be obliged to do so.

Others scorned such a course as pusillanimous, declaring that Great Britain was our "natural" enemy and it was Great Britain that we should fight—very soon.

Still others, in all seriousness, thought and urged that this nation of no experience in international warfare, no military tradition, and virtually no army or navy, should take on *both* of those world powers *at once*. It was, they said, the only honor-able course.

For these John Randolph had only a guffaw.

I am myself in a situation similar to what would have been that of one of the unfortunate people of Caracas, if preadvised of the danger which overhung his country. I know that we are on the brink of some dreadful scourge, some great desolation, some awful visitation from that Power whom, I am afraid, we have in our national capacity taken no pains to conciliate. . . . Go to war without money, without men, without a navy! Go to war when we have not the courage, while your lips utter war, to lay war taxes! when your whole courage is exhibited in passing Resolu-tions! The people will not believe it!

Sam Dana of Connecticut, that slab-sided unsmiling man, in his nasal voice pierced the both-countries proposal:

As to war with Great Britain and France, I should wish
to delay that till I could understand how it was with two
nations at war with each other. I should like first to make
some enquiry on the subject. I wish to know if any gentleman of military talents has drawn up any system of fighting
three armies together. One against two on the same side, is
no new thing, sir, but three against each other is a perfect
novelty. I really do not know how they could draw up
their troops in order of battle, supposing three armies to
meet. They could not be drawn up in parallel lines, for
each army must be opposed to two others. It is a sort of
prismatic or *triangular* thing; for I cannot take three lines
and form a square of them, or any other regular body.
How would they form a line of reserve? The only way that
I can think of arranging an army on this principle, was to
draw up the three armies in a triangular form, the angles
at 120 degrees, the whole making 360 degrees, or a whole
circle; but in this case you must keep them there, not let
them move, or you destroy the principle. This is a new
thing, which I wish to have explained. It is not the old
fashioned way of fighting at all.

This, then, was the situation in 1811 when the War Hawks
swooped upon Washington.

Chapter 5

THERE WAS IN all truth something accipitrine about them. Clay,
Calhoun, William Lowndes, Langdon Cheves, square-jawed
Felix Grundy, Johnson of Kentucky, Troup of Georgia, Potter
of New York—they were all young, the oldest being thirty-six;
they were lawyers; they were smart; they were impatient. There

might be wide differences of temperament among them—Calhoun of South Carolina, for instance, was an implacable, stolid man, without humor, who (the son of an unlettered immigrant) was determinedly aristocratic; while Henry Clay of Kentucky, though he had winged his man in a duel, and though he was almost pathetically eager to be popular, loved late hours and high stakes (he could hold his liquor and usually won) and could not resist cracking the whip of his wit in such a way as to impair his chances of the presidency. ("You, sir," a long-winded old General Smyth cried at him on the floor of Congress, "speak for the present generation; but *I* speak for posterity." To which Clay replied: "Yes, and you seem resolved to speak until the arrival of your audience." Now, you don't win electoral votes that way.)

The eleventh had been a do-little Congress, wobbling, vacillating, teetering at the edge of war, its collective breath held. Thanks to the War Hawks the twelfth was quite otherwise. These young men knew what they wanted, and they meant to get it. Of them alone it could be said, and was said, that they *sought* this war. They *worked for* it. They were not interested in seamen's rights. Paper blockades and the doctrine of continuous voyage concerned them not at all. What they wanted was—land.

The War Hawks came from the West and the South, or if from the North they came from the western part of it (Potter, who was to be made head of the all-important Ways and Means Committee of the new House, represented the extreme western part of New York State, which was virtually the frontier). They were touchy about Indians, or said that they were. It is difficult to see why. The Creeks of the South, while numerous as red men went, were anything but formidable. In the valley of the Ohio, where the clamor for war was loudest, there were only six scattered tribes, the largest of them, the Shawnees, numbering fewer than 1,000, while the whole lot put together—and they never *were* put together—couldn't have been more than 5,000. Pushed back, badly armed when they were armed at all, broken into tiny unfortified villages, the Indians of the Ohio River valley could be ferocious sporadically, individually, when they were drunk, but taken as a whole they could not be thought of as a menace to the almost one million whites in that valley, a large percentage of whom were able-bodied males, and all armed.

The War Hawks cried that the British were backing the Indians of the Ohio Valley, something the British denied. The War Hawks said that the Hudson's Bay Company was monopolizing the fur trade and supplying the redskins with muskets, which the Hudson's Bay Company denied. The War Hawks asserted that the British encouraged Tecumseh and his odd brother, Lawlewatkau or Elkswatawa or Tenskwatawa (it means Open Door any way), commonly known as The Prophet, in their attempts to organize a federation opposed to the further encroachment of white men upon Indian territory; and it was true that the British did coddle Tecumseh a bit, making him, among other things, a brigadier general in their army; but any Westerner surely knew that Prophet or no Prophet, Tecumseh or no Tecumseh, and no matter what contributions the British might make, the redskins never would get together and stay together, for they simply were not that kind of people.

The War Hawks, bluntly, wanted Canada.

Upper Canada was a vast sprawling indeterminate wilderness north of the Great Lakes, its capital York (the present Toronto), and its white inhabitants, very thinly spread, being mostly from the United States, the so-called Late Loyalists, frontiersmen who for one reason or another preferred to live and work under the British crown. It was thought that those settlers, all of them recent, would be sympathetic to an invasion. If Upper Canada could be won—and it should be an easy conquest—the frontiersman of the Ohio Valley could push the Indians still farther north and west, moving on himself when his fields wore out.

Lower Canada, the province called Quebec, which included New Brunswick and Nova Scotia, could come later. Its population was largely French and was believed to hate England.

The War Hawks were quick to point out that the militia of both Canadas was weak and that there were very few regular troops stationed there, while the mother country, engaged in a life-or-death struggle 3,000 miles away, could not be expected to send more. The War Hawks would add that the total population of both Canadas was scarcely half a million, while the population of the United States was almost eight million. So—what were we waiting for? [8]

The general policy of expansion of course would be approved by the Southerners, who had their eyes on East Florida, presently an alarming haven for escaped slaves.

So serene an observer as the sage of Monticello, surely no Hawk, believed that in the event of war the taking of Quebec would be "a mere matter of marching," and could be accomplished the first summer, while the following year Halifax would fall, marking "the final expulsion of England from the American continent."

In Congress they were even more cocky.

"The conquest of Canada is in your power," Clay told the House. "I trust I shall not be deemed presumptuous when I state that I verily believe that the militia of Kentucky are alone competent to place Montreal and Upper Canada at your feet."

"I believe that in four weeks from the time that a declaration of war is heard on our frontiers the whole of Upper Canada and a part of Lower Canada will be in our possession," solemnly averred the solemn John Caldwell Calhoun.

"This war, if carried on successfully," said Grundy, who was comparatively cautious, "will have its advantages. We shall drive the British from our continent."

Nor need it be too costly to "our continent"; and it could even be made to pay.

"We should be able in a short time to remunerate ourselves tenfold for all the spoliations she [Great Britain] has committed on our commerce," Potter declared.

There was one dissenting voice, a familiar one.

"Ever since the report of the Committee on Foreign Relations came into the House we have heard but one word—like the whippoorwill, but one monotonous note—Canada, Canada, Canada!" cried John Randolph.[9]

The War Hawks were florid orators, in the tradition of the time, but they did more than just make speeches. They believed in direct action; and while the story of a Congressional group calling upon Madison with the threat that if he didn't demand war he would not be re-elected can be put aside as slander, it is significant that such a story was told—and by some believed.

The War Hawks were the first to see the enormous power inherent in the speakership of the House. They demanded, dickered for, and got this post for their leader, Henry Clay, who was then thirty-four. Clay immediately and unblushingly appointed War Hawks to all the important chairmanships.

So they were in the saddle, these bright young men. And they meant to ride hard.

Chapter 6

THOUGH WAR HAD been years in coming, when it did come it startled everybody. For so long a time had the fuse been sputtering that folks began to believe that the bomb never would explode.

The first of June, 1812, President Madison, having prepared the way by means of a special ninety-day embargo calculated to keep American ships in their home ports rather than permit them to be seized in various parts of the world by the ubiquitous British when war was declared—but the secret had not been well kept, and vessels flocked out of American ports by the score just before the embargo went into effect—sent a special message to Congress.

He stressed impressment, "this crying enormity, which Great Britain would be so prompt to avenge if committed against herself," though he waxed even more vitriolic over the orders-in-council.

The farmer was not forgotten:

> . . . our commerce has been plundered in every sea, the great staples of our country have been cut off from their legitimate markets, and a destructive blow aimed at our agricultural and maritime interest.

That last phrase must have been especially startling to the wheat raisers and shippers, who had found a new and lucrative market in the armies, British, Spanish, and Portuguese, that England was maintaining in the Iberian peninsula. However, they were to go right on with this trade even after war had been declared, working under special licenses, since Britain needed the grain—and America the money.

Great Britain was chided for having repudiated Erskine, but nothing was said about the repudiation of the treaty Monroe and Pinkney had framed in London.

The Indians were brushed in, very lightly—"It is difficult to account for the activity and combinations which have for some time been developing themselves among tribes in constant intercourse with British traders and garrisons without connecting their hostility with that influence," though no specific charge was made.

Now and then the old James Madison of *The Federalist* papers would break through:

> It has become, indeed, sufficiently certain that the commerce of the United States is to be sacrificed, not as interfering with the belligerent rights of Great Britain; not as supplying the wants of her enemies, which she herself supplies; but as interfering with the monopoly which she covets for her own commerce and navigation. She carries on a war against the lawful commerce of a friend that she may the better carry on a commerce with an enemy—a commerce polluted by the forgeries and perjuries which are for the most part the only passports by which it can succeed.

With an engaging candor, near the end, and as though he had

just thought of it, President Madison mentioned the fact that the United States of America had also been insulted, again and again, by France. He did not linger over this.

Finally, he called for war against Great Britain.

The House passed this message on to the Committee of Foreign Relations, Congressman Calhoun chairman, which reported the very next day, strongly favoring war. The House decided to debate this report—in secret.

A Massachusetts Federalist, Josiah Quincy, moved that the debate be made public. He was voted down.

John Randolph, remarking that they could all use a little time in which to cool off, moved for a postponement of the debate until November. This too was voted down, overwhelmingly.

The vote a week later astonished nobody familiar with the sectional make-up of the House. It was 79-49 in favor of war. Of the ayes, 48 were from the South or the West, 14 were from Pennsylvania, and only 17 were from north of Pennsylvania. Of the nays, 34 were from Northern states, 2 were from Pennsylvania, 13 were from the South, and there were none at all from the West.

In the Senate, where the vote was 19-13, the division was almost exactly the same.

"Free Trade and Sailors' Rights" was to be the slogan; yet the vast majority of seamen and traders alike came from New England, where the war was fervently resented.

It was much commented upon at the time that the South and West insisted upon defending the North and East, which didn't want to be defended.

June 18, then, Congress sent the resolution to the President, who promptly signed it; and the proclamation [10] was framed and issued that very day by the Attorney General.

By a quirk of fate, just two days before that, June 16, the British Foreign Minister, Castlereagh, had announced to the House of Commons that the government at last had decided to rescind the orders-in-council; and this was actually done a few days later. It made us feel foolish, when the news came. It made the British furious.

The British had been having a hard enough time without this altogether unexpected blow. Whatever else he might have been, Napoleon was a first-class fighting man, relentless, imaginative, quick, and utterly dirty. It was a case of no-holds-barred for anybody who tackled him, and also a case of no chance to catch breath. In addition, just a little while ago the government had been shaken when royal physicians officially declared that the king, George III, who had been subject to fits of madness, now at last was definitely, fully—and legally—insane. This meant that the fat and loathsome Prince of Wales, another George, who was believed to favor the Whigs—the Tories presently were in power—became Prince Regent. "Prinny," as the English public called him, no more affectionately than they called Napoleon "Boney," proved when in power to be much more conservative than anybody had expected; but for a time the government structure of the realm had wobbled, and it had been impossible to take so radical a step as the annulment of the orders-in-council.

Besides all that, and just as the decisive deed was about to be done, another madman, this one not royal, approached Prime Minister Perceval at the entrance of the House of Commons and shot him dead. Once again there was delay.

Whether war would have been averted if those orders-in-council had been stricken out earlier, or if somehow the news could have been carried much faster, nobody ever will know. Madison himself, writing many years later, wallowing in hindsight, and aware that his war had not been popular, thought that it would. Others disagreed.

It is notable, at least, that nothing was done about renouncing the privilege of impressment on the high seas. The revocation never was meant as a gesture of good-will toward the United States. It was not done as a result of any pressure exerted by American representatives, official or otherwise. It was done at the request—nay, the demand—of English merchants whose trade was suffering because of the various retaliatory measures imposed upon it by the Madison administration. The fact that those measures, economic sanctions, caused even more pain to American than to British commerce meant nothing to the merchants of London. It was *they* who brought the pressure for the death of the orders-in-council.

It is notable as well that the revocation was tentative, experimental, the way being left open for the immediate restoration of the orders-in-council if circumstances appeared to suggest this. That is, the principle behind the orders was never denied, nor would it be. The British government wasn't promising anything, and it was not striving to placate its transatlantic cousin.

One thing at least was certain—the rage of the British public. What did this fresh, freckle-faced, snub-nosed little whipper-snapper of a nation think it was? That a people who had failed to fight after the *Chesapeake-Leopard* affair should now, suddenly, at this stage of the game, not merely show their teeth but actually try to bite—it was unbearable!

The proclamation was not regarded in England with any sense of dismay, still less of fear, only with a choking, blinding surge of indignation. It was a filthy trick, that it was. "A stab in the back," was the commonest expression for it, in print and on the street alike. "A stab in the back"—the British public would not soon forget it. Not right now, because there was too much work to be done slugging it out with Boney on the continent, but *soon* the thing would be avenged, and that damned gang of Yankees would be taught a few lessons.

This feeling was not a mere flare-up. It did not immediately ebb. It was to last at least for two and a half years, when it would lead to that gathering at Negril Bay, to the knockout blow.

Chapter 7

IF THERE WAS a place where that explosion raised even more angry echoes than in England it was New England.

Nominally Republican in politics, though not vehemently so, New England yet contained most of what die-hard Federalists were left, and in any event the attitude of its leaders could best be described—leaving party lines aside—as anti-Virginian.

That man Jefferson and all his toadies, Madison, Monroe, the others, must have thought that there was something *indecent* about buying and selling. They were bound and determined, down there in Washington, it would seem, somehow to fashion this country into one for farmers alone. They seemed to think that you could run a shop in Hartford the way you ran a plantation in the Old Dominion. They weren't satisfied with grabbing and keeping for their friends virtually all the jobs in the federal government: they must bend their enemies to their will. First it had been the embargo—or "dambargo," as it was called in New England—and then the non-intercourse act, a system concocted in Richmond or Williamsburg, whereby a man whose politics you didn't like was forced to cut his own commercial throat. Then, with the country reeling along the cliff edge of ruin, there had been some relief for a little while. But soon—another embargo, a new one.

And now—the Lord help us!—war.

There never had been any love lost between the Virginians and the New Englanders, those "wise men of the East." The one-term administration of John Adams, a concession, had been a resounding failure, the last gasp, it would appear, of Federalism. Jefferson and his followers were having everything their own way. And there was an additional complaint, now that the insurging Westerners had made themselves felt. The Westerners were a different people entirely, those men from the other side of the mountains; and they had different interests—and very bad manners. Of course they had taken up with the democratic Jeffersonians. Of course they were in this crisis backing that brash Gallomaniac, that kowtower to the Anti-Christ (as Napoleon was called everywhere east of the Hudson), James Embargo Madison, who chirruped, who squinted. What did they think they were, anyway, to try to grab control of a nation that Massachusetts almost single-handedly had started? In Boston there was much angry talk about "the good old thirteen states."

But there was more than talk. There was a distinct strengthening of Federalism; and the fact that the two parties were now in reverse, the Federalists clamoring for states' rights, the Republicans for a strong central government, caused nobody to laugh—at least nobody in public life, or who hoped to be there. New York elected a Federalist Assembly, and its De Witt Clinton made a deal with the New England Federalists whereby he came within nineteen electoral votes of winning the Presidency from James Madison, who was running for re-election in that year of 1812. Senator Pickering's toast at a dinner in Boston to the insufferable Francis James Jackson, who had just retired (by request) as British ambassador at Washington, "The world's last hope—Britain's fast-anchored isle!" was much quoted. Another popular toast—and it was made in public on more than one occasion—was "The existing war—this child of prostitution—may no American acknowledge it as legitimate!" Nantucket actually proclaimed itself neutral, though nobody paid any attention to that. Massachusetts, which included Maine, elected a Federalist governor, retiring little Elbridge Gerry, the "gerrymander" Gerry, who thereupon became Madison's running-mate in the Presidential election—a maneuver that could not have wooed many votes from New England.

The new governor, Caleb Strong, when war was declared issued a proclamation calling for a fast and for public mourning because of this action taken "against the nation from which we are descended, and which for many generations has been the bulwark of the religion we profess," and even though that last assertion must have set many a Congregationalist back on his heels, flags were put at half-mast all over the state.

Strong, like the governors of Rhode Island and Connecticut, refused to turn his militia over to the federal government or to let it operate outside the state; and when Governor Chittenden of Vermont, who had permitted *his* to go, sought to recall it from the federal service, there was a great deal of talk in Congress—but it came to nothing—of trying him for treason.

Yet it was the militia that the Republicans had depended upon, for they dreaded the thought of a large federal army, or even a small one. The militia was Jeffersonian in its very nature, each man defending his own household. Nothing else would do for this country. "It is nonsense to talk of regulars," Jefferson wrote to Monroe. "They are not to be had among a people so easy and happy as ours. We might as well rely on calling down an army of angels from heaven."

Congress had authorized the President to sign up a hundred thousand volunteers, and this the President had done; but they didn't appear. If you went into the army you were held for five years, the pay, after a $16 bounty, being $5 a month—or about half of what a laborer got—plus, on discharge, three months pay and 160 acres of public land. If you went into the militia not only were you among neighbors but you could not be made to leave the state and your stretch of active service would be no more than six months, perhaps as little as three. A few months after the declaration of war Congress raised a private's pay to $8 a month; but enlistments lagged, and not only in New England but all over the country.

Men and money were needed even to get this war started, and for money Washington quite naturally appealed to Boston, the banking center of the United States. The response was—shoulder blades. The bankers of Philadelphia and New York were cold enough, but those in Boston simply turned their backs. It was bad enough to have to *have* this damned Republican war. They certainly weren't going to help *pay* for it.

In particular that slogan "Free Trade and Sailors' Rights" graveled New England. Were those drooling, pseudo-humanitarian, democratic beefwits in Washington trying to make *them* seem responsible for this war? It looked so.

There had been a certain amount of impressment on the part of the French, and even a bit by the Dutch, but when the Massachusetts House of Representatives, bridling, decided to look into the matter on its own, it was only the allegations against "Britain's fast-anchored isle" that it was interested in, these, after all, making up the great mass of the charges. The Massachusetts House appointed a committee, which scrutinized with an admittedly prejudiced eye the nearest thing to a reliable, definite figure that the whole controversy had as yet thrown up—the figure of 6,057 American seamen impressed into the British Navy, as reported by the Secretary of State, Monroe, to President Madison, who on January 16, 1812, had handed the report on to Congress.

The committee found many duplications, and it implied, though it could not prove, that this meant doctoring. However, six John Smiths would not be too many for a list that long, and in this case every John Smith gave a different address. At this distance it was clearly impossible even to estimate how many of the men on the list were claiming U.S. birth only on the basis of forged and purchased "protections." That practice might not have been as bad as the British claimed it was; but it was bad enough. Moreover, the committee pointed out that it was equally impossible to determine how many of those men were "real" Americans, and how many foreign born. Yankees, on the whole, were not given to serving before the mast. It just didn't pay enough. They might be boys, apprentices, or they might be young men out for the experience; but if they stayed at sea for any mentionable length of time they were likely to be officers, none of whom was ever even threatened with impressment.

Just how serious, after all, *was* this issue of impressment, an issue that might have occupied career diplomats for some years but that only a little while ago had been brought to the attention of the public, and was now, abruptly, given as one of the chief causes of "Mister Madison's War"?

The Massachusetts House committee summoned fifty-one shipowners and took their sworn depositions. (Why they did not summon masters or even mates, who would have been closer to the purported evil—and who certainly were thick in those parts —was never made clear.) The results were sensational.

These men, who employed 1,500 seamen at that time, and had done so for many years, among themselves could remember only thirty-five cases of impressment, only twelve of those being Americans, and nine of the Americans had been discharged after investigation, while a tenth had escaped.

James Perkins and Thomas Handasyde Perkins, his brother and partner, employed between 100 and 150 seamen a year, and only three of these—none an American—ever had been impressed from their vessels. T. H. Perkins further testified that foreigners often asked him for jobs, admitting that they had no certificates of U.S. birth but promising to get those before they sailed: the average "protection" in Boston sold for $2, he said.

The most telling testimony was that of William Gray of Boston, who was not only the largest shipowner in New England but also a Republican. In the forty-odd years of his business experience he could recollect scarcely half a dozen cases of impressment from his ships, and most of those, to the best of his knowledge, were foreigners.

The report of the committee was roundly condemned and as roundly endorsed; but it was read almost everywhere, which did not make the administration happy.[11]

Chapter 8

MICHILIMACKINAC, sometimes called the Gibraltar of the North, was a log fort on an island that controlled the straits between lakes Michigan and Huron; and on the morning of July 17, 1812, the U.S. Army commanding officer there, young Lieutenant Hanks, awoke to find himself surrounded, while a brass cannon leered down upon him from a hill.

Captain Charles Roberts of the British Army, commander of the post at St. Joseph Island, Sault Ste. Marie, sent in a demand of surrender. Hanks studied the layout. He estimated, correctly, that there were four to five hundred men out there, red and white, most of them red. His supplies wouldn't hold him here long; and any resistance meant massacre, scalps. The fortifications, due to the neglect not of Hanks but of his faraway superiors, were paper-weak. He had exactly fifty-seven effectives, besides twenty-odd sick; and he didn't have much ammunition. He surrendered.

He got excellent terms, himself and all his men released on parole. He was never reprimanded, officially or otherwise. After all, why should he have expected an attack? He did not know until that momentous morning that war had been declared, a month before, almost to the day, by the United States against Great Britain. Nobody had taken the trouble to tell him.

There's the way it was with so many of those outlying, half-forgotten posts. The United States Army, at the time it was first called upon to face the might of the "fast-anchored isle," consisted of ten "old" and thirteen "new" regiments. The new ones had been authorized a little earlier by Congress in one of the few acts of military preparation that body did make. They were expected, these new ones, to do most of the fighting; but they were not filling up fast. Not one of the original ten regiments of the regular army was at even half strength. The men in them were poorly equipped, dispiritedly led. They were broken into small groups, neglected, scattered over thousands of miles of wilderness and frontier. They were not expected to do much of the fighting—assuming that it would call for any real fighting to conquer Canada—for they were thought to be indispensable where they were.

There was also, of course, the militia. There was always the militia. The country's original soldier, George Washington, had complained querulously and sometimes harshly about the militia; but never mind that; the militia was an American way of life.

Brigadier General William Hull was sixty years old. He sat in his tent at Fort Detroit, absent-mindedly cramming quid after quid of tobacco into his mouth, so that the brown juice dribbled out of the corners of his lips, staining his beard. He was a badly troubled man. Ever since he had heard of the loss of Michilimackinac from Lieutenant Hanks as Hanks and his men passed through Detroit to the rear to sit out the rest of the war, he had been wondering whether he too shouldn't surrender without a fight. True, he had a much stronger post than Hanks had had, and a much larger command, something close to 2,000, or about as many as the British commander out there, one Isaac Brock.

Brock was forty-two, a soldier who knew his business. He had been notified immediately of the declaration of war, and had gone into prompt action. General Hull, though he was in the field on the other side of the Detroit River and had been expecting news of war at any time, was not notified until several days later. Washington sent him this information *by ordinary mail*. Even the fur traders to the west and the north of him, most of them in Canadian territory, knew about it sooner than General Hull. John Jacob Astor was a great deal faster than the War Department at Washington.

Brock came from the isle of Guernsey. Of French stock, he

had no illusions about gallantry. The thing to do in war, he reasoned, was win. A large proportion of his besieging force consisted of uncertain but fierce Indians. He knew that General Hull knew this. He also knew that General Hull had brought along on this wilderness invasion not only his son, as an aide, but also his daughter and her two small children, the General's grandchildren. There were other children and women inside the walls of Fort Detroit; they had come from the surrounding countryside.

"It is far from my inclination to join in a war of extermination," Brock had written in his demand for surrender, "but you must be aware that the numerous body of Indians who have attached themselves to my troops will be beyond my control the moment the contest commences."

Yes, William Hull knew. He knew what Indians did.

That was August 15.

Hull hadn't wanted this job. As governor of the Territory of Michigan and also as a veteran of the Revolution, despite his age he had made the long trip to Washington, when war clouds began to gather, to offer a plan for the invasion of Upper Canada, a plan that included the building of a navy to control Lake Erie first. The plan was accepted, and he was asked to command the expedition. He declined. It was only after President Madison pleaded with him personally that he had consented to lead the thing. And now he wished he hadn't.

He knew the meaning of that note well enough. He was worried sick, literally.

His plan to build vessels for the control of the lake had been vetoed: such construction would hold up what was meant to be a whirlwind invasion. He should have refused positively to take this command, then and there. He hadn't. And here he was, morosely chewing, drooling, not knowing which way to move, and so not moving at all.

His force was mostly militia, and the officers—he knew it, he sensed it—despised him. As for the colonel of the one federal regiment, the 4th Infantry, he was coldly correct. More than once in the course of that long and terrible trek through the

Black Swamp country, building their own road as they went, there had been mutterings of mutiny. Hull did not know what the officers said—they became clams at his approach—but he did not like the looks he got. He suspected that the colonels, militiamen, mostly from Ohio, had suggested deposing him as an emergency field measure and had asked Lieutenant Colonel Miller of the U.S. 4th to take over the command, something that officer refused to do. Would such men fight, if he called upon them? Was it worth while fighting anyway?

The men of his army had crossed the Detroit readily enough, once they'd been told that a state of war existed, and the General had issued a proclamation that just at first appeared to have a tremendous effect, deserters from the Canadian militia coming in by the dozen, by the score. But the General had been forced to give up his plan of marching upon the unfortified York, capital of Upper Canada. Brock was in the field now, and Brock wasted no time. General Hull was too far from his base. He retreated, back across the river into the United States, and occupied the fort at Detroit, a town of about 800 population, much swollen now by refugees.

The British controlled the river. They had a couple of gunboats, *Hunter* and *Queen Charlotte,* out there right now, blasting away at the fort. Because he had not known of the declaration of war, General Hull, when at last he reached Lake Erie had put all his sick, all his medical supplies, his entrenchment tools, and even his private papers, into an unarmed schooner, *Cuyahoga,* which met him there at the mouth of the Maumee and which he reckoned could carry these things to Detroit ahead of the main party, greatly relieving his overworked men; but the British, who *had* heard of the declaration of war, seized the *Cuyahoga,* supplies, papers, and all, when it would have passed their fort at Malden on the Canadian side of the Detroit River. Was that the General's fault?

Thanks to this seizure, the British knew Hull's exact strength. He was by no means as well informed about them, but he was reasonably sure that they were throwing against him virtually everything they had. A diversion, a feint toward Montreal, say, in the Lake Champlain district, where there were many United States troops, or an invasion of Upper Canada from Niagara or from Sackets Harbor, would save the General and his men, even now. Another veteran of the Revolution, Henry Dearborn, senior major general of the U.S. Army, was in charge at Albany, N.Y., and General Hull, who had heard not a word from him, surely couldn't expect assistance from that quarter. (Dearborn later confessed that though he had held this position for almost half a year he did not until then know that his command extended as far west as Niagara; but even when he did learn this, he did nothing about it, leaving Hull to his fate. Dearborn was sixty-two years old.)

An aide came in to tell William Hull that two companies of Michigan militia—his own men!—had deserted.

A cannonball landed in the yard and mangled four privates. Hull could hear their screams.

". . . Indians who had attached themselves to my troops will be beyond my control. . . ."

His line of supply, almost two hundred miles long, had been threatened, and he had been obliged to send almost half of his force to support it. Now those men were cut off by additional Indians from Amherstburg, and it was a question whether they could battle their way back to the seriously weakened fort where the women and children were.

The General chewed on, silent, seeing no one.

And now the crushing news from Michilimackinac. *That* meant that thousands of Indians from the north and the west soon would be swarming in to join Isaac Brock, who a little while ago had crossed the river into the United States, a force that all but *asked* for a sally, standing as it did only a few hundred yards away, banging with its two- and three-pounders.

The General rose. He sighed, and called for a flag of truce. Without further ado he surrendered.

He surrendered the town and the fort and everything that was in them, and even surrendered the force that was now marching back. He did this without having fired a shot.

At Fort Dearborn (a place that was later to be called Chicago) there was another of those far-flung Army posts, fifty-three men this time. Washington seemingly had forgotten them, but Hull, as commander in the field, had sent them an order to evacuate the fort as soon as possible and join him at Detroit. The day they started to evacuate—it was the very day Hull surrendered at Detroit, August 16—they were set upon by an overwhelming force of British-led Indians. Those who were not killed on the spot were captured; and *they* in turn, as prisoners, were slaughtered that very night when the Indians, drunk, got out of hand —though there is nothing to indicate that their British officers did anything to halt that horrid business. The following day the fort itself was burned to the ground.

That was the situation at the end of the second month of the war. Not only was there not a U.S. soldier anywhere across the border—for Dearborn had not stirred from Albany—but the army of the west had ceased to exist, having been ignominiously surrendered, while all the strategic strong points on the United States side either had been razed or were in the hands of the enemy.

It would seem that the conquest of Canada was not to be "a mere matter of marching," after all.

Chapter 9

THE UPROAR WAS stunning. The nation, for once united, raised a howl of indignation and fury. Nobody had a good word to say for William Hull, that craven, that traitor, who was compared—when he wasn't compared with the Devil himself—with Benedict Arnold. No wonder the war had started badly, with men like that in command of armies.

It is remarkable that the United States could think of no

other way to explain the disaster except by betrayal. What possible reason William Hull would have had, after leaving his job as governor of Michigan, to accept any sort of bribe from the British—or for that matter, what possible reason the latter would have to *offer* a bribe—was never brought up. But Hull was. The War Department charged him with treason, cowardice, neglect of duty, and unofficer-like conduct.

Almost immediately it became clear that there might be trouble assembling a court, since most of the officers of sufficient rank to sit in judgment on Hull, themselves were in similar or somewhat similar straits.

It was planned to hold the proceedings in Philadelphia, February 25, 1813: the sooner the better, was the official position, since the public was clamoring for blood. But Major General Wade Hampton, a comparatively young man—he was fifty-seven —came to be under a professional cloud because of his intense hatred of General Wilkinson; and though charges never were pressed against Hampton—because of his resignation, the acceptance of which in itself constituted an acquittal—yet the Hull court-martial had to be postponed. Bumbling indecisive old Henry Dearborn, the senior ranking major general of the whole army, had to be recalled from his New York command to face charges, in a court of inquiry, of having done nothing whatsoever; and obviously he would not be the man to preside at the trial of William Hull, who, had it not been for the dillydallying of Dearborn, might not have been where he was. The second ranking major general, Thomas Pinckney, was not at the moment facing any sort of charges, perhaps because at the age of sixty-three he was too tired to get into trouble; but he was needed in the south, or thought he was. As for that windbag Wilkinson, brought up from New Orleans, he had made a monumental fiasco of a second attempted invasion of Canada, from New York State, and he too, as a candidate for court-martial, was not available.

At last, and in spite of the cloud over his head, General Dearborn, recalled from active duty on the border—if it could be called active—was appointed commanding officer of the new

New York City military district *and* presiding officer of the Hull court-martial. This appointment was much criticized; but in the long run probably it made no difference. Any court-martial at that time would have found William Hull guilty, as this one did March 26, 1814, almost two years after the event. The ridiculous charge of treason was dropped, but the defendant was convicted of all the other charges, and sentenced to be shot.

On April 25 President Madison approved the sentence but remitted its execution. Hull's name was ordered stricken from the army roll. He didn't live much longer, having nothing to live for. The public never forgave him.[12]

The hatred that New Englanders had for Virginians, politically at least, was as nothing to the feeling New Yorkers had for them; and this was reciprocal. The Virginians not only were gentlemen, but *country* gentlemen. They lolled. Carefully they went in for carelessness of dress. They knew one another. They were all Episcopalians. Such men not only disliked but deeply distrusted the representatives of big city machine politics; and members of the Society of St. Tammany [13] felt that same way about the la-di-das of Virginia, with all their hounds and their horses.

A Cabinet shake-up clearly was called for by the surrender at Detroit, and the first heads to fall naturally would be those of the Secretary of War and the Secretary of the Navy, both, even by peacetime standards, bunglers. When Madison replaced Paul Hamilton by William Jones of Pennsylvania as head of the Navy there were no hisses, if there was no applause either; but a scream rose, a series of screams, when with a perfectly straight face he nominated as Secretary of War in the place of the amiable but almost unbelievably incompetent Dr. Eustis of Boston, his friend and friendly rival, James Monroe, who was already Secretary of State and was not to be called upon to relinquish that post.

This was too much. *Another* Virginian! Not only New York but all the North disapproved, loudly, though New York was the loudest. Monroe was tall, old-fashioned in his dress but not in his ideas, ambitious, an experienced diplomat, a veteran of the Revolution. He got things done. No doubt he would have made an excellent Secretary of War, as he proved during the two months late in 1812 and early in 1813 when he actually did hold down both posts; but this was not to be.

"If this war's got to be fought in our front yard, as it looks like," New York said, in effect, "then we ought to have something to say about who directs it."

The logic, from a political point of view, was unassailable. Though it was against his better judgment, James Madison bowed his head. New York could have the job.

There were two possibilities. The governor, Daniel D. Tompkins, was not well known in Washington, where for that very reason he would have been preferred to Senator John Armstrong, who was. But Tompkins elected to stay in New York for the present, and he had his eyes on the Presidency. Armstrong fancied himself as a military man. He and the President were members of the same party, though not members of the same set, and it pained Madison to appoint him; but he bowed to political necessity, slave to duty that he was; and the Senate, without any enthusiasm—the vote was 18-15—confirmed the nomination.

Secretary of State Monroe wouldn't even speak to the man. It must have made the Cabinet meetings unpleasant.

The American was to prove that he wasn't a poor soldier, but at this time undoubtedly his officers were poor officers, and perhaps because of what he took over—the paper mess, low morale, Dearborn's doddering, Detroit and the mandatory court-martial of Hull, the Wilkinson-Hampton feud—it was some time before Armstrong could allow his common sense to assert itself.

The U.S. Army had started at the wrong end. Upper Canada was wilderness. There were no roads. The settlements there could be supplied only by way of the St. Lawrence and the lower lakes. Cut the St. Lawrence, and Upper Canada would fall by itself. The place to strike was Quebec, or, if this was thought too strong—and it *was* strong—then hit Montreal, higher up the river, that city to which Lake Champlain deliberately pointed, as though calling it to our attention. Montreal would be much more readily reached than Detroit. And even more accessible, a wonderfully easy place to keep supplied, was the upper St. Lawrence, where the river falls out of Lake Ontario. The southern bank of the river, which is narrow at this point, was U.S. property anyway. A handful of men there with a few cannons could sever Upper Canada's lifeline. No invasion would be called for.

Even Dearborn saw this, and proposed it; but he did nothing about it. Hull's energy—he had performed engineering prodigies on his journey to Detroit—together with the supposed enthusiasm of the men out that way for a war nobody else seemed to care for—probably had been the reason for the western stroke. *Now* the reason was revenge, a poor one from the military point of view.

In time the ordinarily pig-headed Armstrong let himself be persuaded: he "eventually submitted to the superior ignorance of his colleagues," and approved another advance into Upper Canada with a stab at Montreal only as a feint. "Thus the object which should have been primary was made secondary, and that which should have been secondary was made primary, according to the approved practice of the amateur strategist." [14]

Detroit actually was retaken, if without any glory. Perhaps the Navy had something to do with this western movement, though truly the Navy had not been concerned with the original fall of Detroit. There had come to Lake Ontario Commodore Isaac Chauncey of Connecticut, with instructions to build as many ships as he could, for now everybody saw that control of the Great Lakes, and in particular of the two smaller, lower, more easterly lakes, Ontario and Erie, would be necessary to any victory. Chauncey persuaded Dearborn, who by that time had learned that his command stretched this far, that the thing to do was capture York first, since the side that held York controlled the lake; and Kingston, at the beginning of the St. Lawrence River—that is, at the easternmost end of Lake Ontario—could wait until later.

Armstrong agreed, it is hard to see why.

York was taken easily enough, but it was an expensive success. The garrison put up a spirited fight; scores of U.S. soldiers, including Zebulon Montgomery Pike, a man known to posterity as the discoverer and namer of a certain mountain peak but known to those around him as "the best brigadier in the service," were killed in the accidental explosion of a powder magazine; so that the capture of York cost as much, almost, as a major battle. And it wasn't decisive. It didn't prove anything. The shipyard was burned, and some supplies too were destroyed—those that couldn't be carried back in the already overcrowded ships. One ship was captured, but a much larger one had departed only a few days before. Clearly York could not be held: nobody, unless it was Commodore Chauncey, ever had dreamed of holding it anyway. The loss of Pike more than off-balanced the petty prestige to be gained by the sacking of a provincial capital. Worst of all, the government buildings at York were burned—apparently by irresponsible soldiers, since Dearborn insisted that it was done without his knowledge and against his orders. This burning, a wanton outrage, with no military motive behind it, was to have black and bitter consequences.

By now it was too late to do anything about Kingston, which had been reinforced, and the original design against Montreal had to be dusted off and put into action. Unfortunately James Wilkinson was the general the prevailing rigid military system forced upon Armstrong for this exploit, and Wilkinson was even worse than usual, so that another year was lost, while Canada, despite her flagrant weaknesses, remained intact.

By the time John Armstrong had really got the situation well in hand he had outworn his usefulness and was obliged to step down.

He had, however, done one fine thing. By various means, but ruthlessly, he had got rid of those superannuated fuddyduddies with whom the Army was cluttered, and had brought forth and promoted much younger, abler men—men like Scott, Izard, and the incomparable Jacob Brown, that Quaker schoolteacher who had a real flair for war. Brown was thirty-eight, Izard thirty-six, Scott twenty-seven.

But the greatest general the U.S. Army was to find in this crisis was a Westerner, and unexpectedly he came out of the militia—the Tennessee militia. His name was Andrew Jackson.

Chapter 10

THE NAVY was different.

This had been planned as a land war. British naval superiority *in American waters,* as of June 1812, was 85 to 14; and the British could bring up many more, for they had in operation 191 ships of the line (the United States had none) and 245 frigates and other vessels (of which the United States had 24). The British had nearby bases—Bermuda, Jamaica, Halifax—and since for all practical purposes they had for some time been blockading American shores anyway it would be an easy matter to draw the strings tight.

The Republicans never had favored a large navy; and such war vessels as the United States did have—good vessels, though not all of them were in good condition at the outbreak of war— had been built by the Federalists. The most that Jefferson's party had consented to do was build a large number of the so-called "gunboats." These were designed for purely defensive purposes, stand-off actions in shallow water. They were cheap, and looked it, cut out as though by a huge cookie-cutter, each being 50 feet long, mounting one miserable cannon, and with a crew of twenty-five. These gunboats were low in the water, with almost no freeboard, and in any sea they rolled so badly that they couldn't shoot. There might have been 200 of them, peppered all over the place. One frigate would have been better. Or a couple of sloops.[15]

In the circumstances it might be expected that the Navy

would consist of resentful place-holders, disgruntled men who served without imagination, without hope. The very opposite was true. Unlike the Army—for brush wars with the Indians didn't count—the Navy had been called upon for some conflict in recent years. There was the war against the Barbary pirates, in the Mediterranean, and also the undeclared naval war against France. Later still there had been the sight and sometimes the sound of those insolent, overbearing British. The *Chesapeake* affair would not soon be forgotten. It rankled; and the nerves of the naval officers were edgy, as was shown by the *President–Little Belt* set-to.

This had been before the war. It was May 16, 1811. *Guerriere* and *Melampus,* a couple of British frigates active off the American coast—it was from *Melampus* that the four men who brought about the *Chesapeake* incident had deserted—were busy near Sandy Hook, stopping American vessels. The Secretary of the Navy, Hamilton, ordered Commodore John Rodgers of the 44-gun frigate *President,* at Annapolis, to sail to New York and investigate—specifically to learn, if possible, whether Captain Dacres of *Guerriere* had impressed a seaman named Diggio [16] from an American brig, a merchantman.

No longer did any American vessel of war put out with her guns off. Moreover, those guns had been modernized for quicker firing. Match tubs and loggerheads no longer were used. There were locks on the cannons *President* carried.

May 16, toward noon, off Cape Henry, they sighted a vessel they took to be *Guerriere,* though she showed no colors. She was certainly a vessel of war, and when she started away from *President* it seemed expedient to give chase.

This pursuit started briskly enough, but after a while the wind fell off, so that it was after seven o'clock, and getting very dark indeed, by the time *President* overhauled the stranger. Rodgers still believed her to be *Guerriere.* Now she showed colors—Rodgers had done so from the beginning of the chase—but nobody on the American vessel could be sure of what they were. Neither vessel had answered the other's signals. It was sure that neither knew. They belonged, at least, to different navies.

All guns had been run out. Every man was at his post.

The vessels stood off and on, as cautious as a couple of strange cats in an alley.

It was a little after eight o'clock when Rodgers hailed. *"What ship is that?"* If he heard no answer it was probably because the other skipper had hailed him at the same time.

A pause.

Then the shooting started.

It was like a barroom brawl. Everybody argued, afterward, about who had thrown the first punch.

There was no question about who threw the last punch. The stranger was silenced in a matter of minutes. Rodgers hailed her again, and got a reply that she was a British vessel of war in distress. He stood by all night, ready to put over boats if signaled. Not until dawn did he see what he had hurt—not the 36-gun *Guerriere* but a mere corvette of 20 guns, less than half the strength of *President*. This was the *Little Belt,* out of Bermuda with dispatches for Dacres of the *Guerriere*. The mistake was a natural one, given the circumstances. *Little Belt's* top hamper, her exceptional spread of canvas, her great length for a corvette, the way she hung her hammocks, and the darkness that had made it impossible to see that she had only one tier of guns— these had to be taken into account. The fight could scarcely have ended any other way. What was interesting about it was Rodgers' willingness to overhaul on the high seas and to question a British vessel of war, no matter how many or how few her guns. What right had he to do that? This was England's ocean, wasn't it?

The scrape served to whet even further the U.S. Navy's eagerness for combat, though in truth the men already, from captains down to mess boys—there were no admirals, and the title "commodore" was honorary—already were razor-sharp.

It could be significant that the average age of those captains was thirty-seven, as compared with the average age of the generals of the Army—fifty-eight.

The United States Navy was not supposed to fight. It was only supposed to back into the various harbors along the coast and thus to cost the British Navy a large number of blockading ships, which would have to be resupplied and replaced from time to time. But fighting was just what the Navy wanted. And fighting was just what it got—for a little while.

There was never any thought of a fleet action; but the American captains refused to remain bottled in harbor, and every time they got a chance, with or without orders, they slipped out to sea. They could hold the open sea for a long while; and though the pickings were petty, and though they got few prizes, their very existence and the possibility that one of them might show up almost anywhere, preoccupied a large part of the British Navy.

One way to whip your enemy was to make him wonder where you were.

There was always the chance—this did not appear to exert any force among American strategists but it was very much in the minds of the British admiralty—that some considerable portion of the French fleet might break out of its ports. Until the entrance of the United States into the war this would have delighted the British Navy, which would smash the enemy piece by piece, first taking the precaution to close her ports against retreat. Now, however, such French warships, perhaps conducted by the unpredictable, dangerous, fast American frigates, having scurried across the Atlantic, might take refuge in some American port, where they would be an even greater nonfighting nuisance because of the supply distance. That meant an increase in the already overstrained British blockading fleet along the French coast.

Any one of those Yankee frigates might appear at any moment anywhere in the world. This disconcerting but inescapable thought raised hob with insurance rates. What if an American vessel was lucky enough to intercept one of the East Indiamen, those immense floating treasure houses? Such a take would spell catastrophe at home. Or—one might appear unexpectedly right in the middle of one of the lightly escorted supply convoys on its way from England to the armies England maintained on the Spanish peninsula. Until this time, the admiralty, with only an occasional hit-and-run French privateer to worry about, had not used large vessels to guard this run; but now, clearly, these escorts must be increased.

An example: Wellington, not the worrying type, late in 1812 was worried breathless about an overdue shipment of many thousands of pairs of shoes for his almost barefoot soldiers. A privateer wouldn't trouble himself with shoes—privateers were interested only in quickly cashable goods and of course cash itself—but an American warship captain would see their military value and confiscate them. It may seem silly from an armchair, but it wasn't silly to Wellington. If those shoes did not arrive (they did) it could cost the war.

Communications never were reliable, but with those American frigates roving the seas at random, likely to pop up anywhere, what might not happen to dispatches? These usually were carried in small fast vessels, corvettes or light brigs, and such a vessel usually could show her heels to any frigate, even one of the U.S. frigates; but who could be sure that the winds would be light? Under a press of canvas the frigate could bear down on the dispatch boat, and seize its papers or cause them to be destroyed, in either event bringing about a change in plans that London wouldn't hear about for at least a month.

Then there was the West Indian run, so much longer than that to Portugal, yet equally vital. That too had to be strengthened, stringent regulations made against any merchanter sailing alone. Making up convoys was a vexatious, time-wasting, money-wasting process—but necessary again now, even after Trafalgar, because of those bloody Yanks.

The public did not know much about this, or didn't care. The public, starved for heroes, only bubbled about the spectacular aspects of the work the U.S. Navy did—that is, the single-ship encounters, the duels. These started early, and came all in a rush.

Chapter 11

THE FIRST THREE weeks of this war Isaac Hull, master of the 44-gun frigate *Constitution,* fretted at Annapolis, completing his crew. Recruits for the U.S. Navy were hard to come by. In the midst of the war scare of 1810 the Navy Department had arranged for a two-year enlistment term, an offer that had worked very well at the time, filling the ships; but now these enlistment terms were running out, and just when the men were most needed they were refusing to sign up for more service, being eager to get into privateering with its possibility of big profits.

Hull was anxious to get to sea for two reasons. First, he might be ordered by Washington to stay where he was, pursuant to the defensive policy of the department. Second, even if he didn't get such an order a British fleet might appear at any hour and force him to stay there by blocking the entrance of Chesapeake Bay, an easy thing to do.

When at last he did get out he ran north, it being his hope to pick up some prizes off the mouth of the St. Lawrence. In this season there should be a great deal of traffic there.

Off a bleak bare sandy island along the southern coast of New Jersey (the present Atlantic City) he fell in with no fewer than five vessels. That was at sundown, and he couldn't be sure who they were. Not until daylight did he learn—for they were still there. They were British frigates, all five of them, *Guerriere, Belvidera, Africa, Shannon, Aeolus,* the expected fleet, the very vessels he had feared would bottle him up in Chesapeake Bay.

Still heading north, Hull cracked on everything but the cook's shirt. The Britishers did the same.

That race, a classic, lasted two nights and three whole days. Repeatedly Hull was almost within gunshot, and several attempts were made to reach him, but he pulled away. He played every trick—balancing the guns, pumping out water, towing, kedging, catching each cupful of wind.

Once a Yankee merchant vessel put in toward them, and the British admiral, Broke, ran up a United States flag—a common *ruse de guerre*—in the hope of enticing the merchantman in to where it could be captured without breaking the pursuit; but Hull immediately hoisted a British flag, and the merchantman ran.

At last Hull shook them off, and when a few days later he sailed into Boston Harbor—which, as he had guessed, was not blockaded—he was given a noisy welcome. Here was the first real news of the war, and it was good. The chase had been a superb display of seamanship, and as such a heartening tale to tell.

Hull would not have put into Boston at all, save for one thing. He had been at sea only eight days, and his provisions were sound, but in the course of the chase he had pumped out ten tons of drinking water, and he needed to replenish his tanks. He got away again as soon as he could. He sailed August 2. The very next day an order came from Washington for him to stay in port.

He cruised off the Banks for a few weeks, picking up sundry prizes, and then, on a southerly course, hundreds of miles from land, in that vast empty ocean—he ran into *Guerriere*.

The English frigate had been detached from Admiral Broke's squadron and was on her way to Halifax for supplies. She was rated as one of the best in the British service. Her master, Dacres, must have known that he was outgunned—there never had been anything secret about these matters—for *Constitution*, though in the complicated system of the day she was rated as a 44-gun vessel, actually carried 55 guns, while *Guerriere*, officially a 36-gunner, carried 49. Even more telling was the respective sizes of the crews. Dacres had 282 men, Hull 456. That *Constitution's* cannons would be well handled could be taken for granted: the Americans always had stressed gunnery. But besides the gunners, Captain Hull would have reserves who could be called upon at any moment to cut away rigging or spars, put out fires, repel boarders or do some boarding of their own, pass up powder, even, in a pinch, to replace the gun handlers.

Dacres was the last man in the world to run away from a fight, but it probably never even occurred to him to do so anyway. A refusal to meet *Constitution*—it was coming on night, and he might have been able to escape under cover of darkness —would have meant a court-martial for Dacres, maybe a firing squad. There was more to it than that. Dacres was only twenty-eight, but he was a seasoned seaman, the son of an admiral, and imbued with the almost hysterical confidence of a British naval officer. To turn from a fight simply because the odds were against you, because you were outclassed, would be unthinkable. Time and again British war vessels had defeated bigger opponents. It had to be that way. This was not vainglory: it was a fixed, superstitious belief.

So they stripped to their battle canvas—jibs, topsails, topgallants—and hoisted their colors, beat to quarters, ran out their guns, spread their nettings, sanded their decks.

For almost two hours they jockeyed for position. Then *Constitution*, having the weather gauge, spread all her canvas and drove straight for *Guerriere*.

This was unorthodox. It was unprecedented. Dacres, watching it, must have gasped. He never could have spared the men to make such a maneuver at such a time, even if he had thought of it.

Hull, mindful of the failing light, had decided to get in close and slug it out toe-to-toe.

Dacres asked nothing better, and in a few minutes they were cruising side by side less than half a pistol shot apart, each giving the other broadside after broadside.

There could be no further raking, in this position, but again and again *Constitution* hulled *Guerriere* between wind and water, so that the British ship fairly reeled, wobbling. A lucky shot from *Guerriere* did start a fire aboard the *Constitution*, but this was quickly put out. Some of *Guerriere's* balls penetrated, though without doing much damage, but many were imbedded in *Constitution's* wooden walls, and a few, these mostly from the topside carronades, literally bounced off *Constitution's* gunwales, causing an American salt to shout: "God damn, she's got iron sides!"

Another salt, on the same side, when he saw *Guerriere's* mizzen knocked down, cried: "We've made a brig of the bastard!"

That smashing of the Britisher's mizzen could be called the "break" of this battle, which lasted less than half an hour. Struck at the base, the mizzen fell across the counter, trailing to leeward, thus forming a sort of murderous sea anchor that caused *Guerriere* to yaw to windward, so that her bowsprit and jibboom fouled the lee mizzen rigging of *Constitution*. For some reason—lack of men?—it appeared to be impossible for the Britishers to cut this mast away; and *Guerriere*—by that time not much more than matchwood anyway—was unmanageable.

That bowsprit, however, might be a perfect boarding plank. On the afterdeck of *Constitution* Lieutenant Morris of the Navy and Lieutenant Bush of the Marines started to pass out boarding pikes and cutlasses. They were both killed, shot from the *Guerriere* tops. Others leapt to replace them.

There was no need. *Guerriere* was only the pulp of a ship now. Dacres fired a gun to leeward, a signal that he meant to strike. Both vessels became silent, while the indifferent smoke, languidly graceful, floated away.

The Union Jack came down.

There was nothing to do about the loser. The British crew, wounded and sound, were transferred to *Constitution*. As was the custom, the dead were shoved overside. Hull sent an officer back aboard the *Guerriere* to get from the captain's cabin the Bible Dacres' mother had given to him years ago. But *Guerriere* couldn't be towed. She had to be burned.

Chapter 12

WHEN HULL GOT back to Boston with his prisoners the whole country was pitched into a frenzy of delight.

Nor was it long before other news came from the sea, to keep this delight at boil.

Captain David Porter in the frigate *Essex* off Bermuda one night had a brush with a sloop-of-war, *Minerva,* which was escorting seven transports of British soldiers from the French West Indies, where since the British victories they were no longer needed, to Canada, where they were. The night was dark, and neither skipper was sure whom or how much he was fighting. *Minerva* got away; but *Essex* did manage to cut out one of the transports, complete with 200 redcoats. *Essex* went on to take eight more prizes, and then another British sloop-of-war.

Alert, on convoy duty, lived up too well to her name, saucily approaching *Essex* to see what she was. *Essex* poured two broadsides into her—and then she knew. *Alert* struck. There wasn't anything else she could have done, outclassed as she was. And now Porter was back in New York with his ten bright prizes.

The *Essex-Alert* meeting took place August 3. October 17 the U.S. sloop *Wasp* met another British convoying sloop, *Frolic,* off Bermuda. It was dirty weather, following a storm in which *Frolic* had been mauled and *Wasp* none too well treated. Nevertheless they went right at it, hammer and tongs. These were bantamweights now—very fast hard fighters. *Frolic* went after the rigging, *Wasp,* a body puncher, after the hull. The seas were running so high that the muzzles of the guns often were dipped into water, and many of the shots must have been misses. This went on for forty-three noisy minutes, neither side giving an inch; until at last, helpless, a mass of splinters, *Frolic* struck.

It had been an inspiriting contest clear through, the odds being about even. True, a few hours later a ship of the line, H.M.S. *Poictiers,* 74 guns, came over the horizon, bound from Halifax for Bermuda, and *Wasp,* even after she had dropped her prize, was too badly crippled to escape, and had to strike before this giant. But the glory remained.

October 25 the frigate *United States,* under Stephen Decatur, off the Azores, met the frigate *Macedonian* of His Majesty's Navy, and outsailed and outslugged her, leaving her a battered wreck. *United States* did have a slight advantage in guns and men, but by no means an advantage so great as to account for *Macedonian's* casualties, nine times those of *United States.*

December 13, *Constitution,* from now on to be called *Old Ironsides,* under the command of William Bainbridge, accompanied by the sloop *Hornet,* David Lawrence, master, appeared off the harbor of San Salvador, Brazil. *Hornet* went in, to find a British sloop-of-war, *Bonne Citoyenne.* They were perfectly matched; and Lawrence, precisely as if this was a café in Heidelberg and not the coast of South America, challenged the British skipper to step outside—beyond the three-mile limit —and fight. The *Bonne Citoyenne* carried a large supply of specie, and so her master refused.

Lawrence himself went outside, hoping that the Britisher would change his mind. Commodore Bainbridge from *Constitution* did what he could to promote the match, actually sending in a message to the British captain, through the U.S. consul at San Salvador, giving his word of honor that he would not interfere when the two sloops engaged. Even then the Britisher (who must have been a cad) refused.

Constitution sailed on. Lawrence, still hoping that the skipper of the *Bonne Citoyenne* would change his mind (he didn't), lingered a little longer, and then he made for Dutch Guiana, which at that time was in the hands of the British. He captured a British brig, a merchantman, with considerable specie aboard. He poked into the Demerara River. He was about to quit the Main and make for the West Indies, when he found himself confronted by the gun brig *Peacock*, R.N. He beat *Peacock* so emphatically that she couldn't be kept afloat, and several of the American seamen sent aboard of her to try to patch her were carried down and drowned.

Meanwhile, Bainbridge, on December 29, the wind being northeast, met the British frigate *Java*, on her way from Spithead to the East Indies, together with a prize she had lately taken, the U.S. merchantman *William*, which for the ensuing two hours simply stayed off to one side and watched the fight.

It was quite a fight.

It began with a series of lunges and parries, as though these two, Bainbridge and Captain Henry Lambert, were expert fencers, each armed with an épée. *Java* was fast. She had been French, a prize, and all the French warships were fast, much faster than those of Great Britain, even faster than the American warships, some of which had been taken off French lines. *Java*, also, had many carronades, good for infighting but not for distance work; and so, understandably, she tried to close. Bainbridge coolly kept away, his gunnery superior. But when he was ready he went in.

From Bainbridge's journal:

At forty minutes past two, determined to close with the enemy notwithstanding his raking. Set the fore and mainsail and luffed up close to him. At fifty minutes past two the enemy's jib-boom got foul of our mizzen rigging. At three the head of the enemy's bowsprit and jib-boom were shot away by us. At five minutes past three, shot away the enemy's foremast by the board. At fifteen minutes past three, shot away his main top mast just above the cap. At forty minutes past three shot away the gaff and spanker boom. At fifty-five minutes past three shot away his mizzenmast nearly by the board.[17]

Java staggered, one-third of her crew dead or dying, her captain unconscious, scarcely a stick left standing in her. She surrendered only when she had to, and indeed all the next day was spent in striving to keep her afloat; but the day after that, the job being given up, she was burned. That was the last day of 1812.

Now, all this was very exciting. The country, which had so badly needed a hero, got a whole glittering procession of them.

Even when the record was broken, when David Lawrence, then in command of *Chesapeake,* permitted himself to be coaxed out of Boston Harbor by the captain of the offstanding *Shannon,* before his green crew had been trained or even organized—even then, and after Lawrence had been severely beaten, the American public persisted in draping these encounters with glory.

Lawrence's dying words, "Don't give up the ship" (which they did, a moment later), were quoted everywhere, a national war cry, as exhilarating as "Don't shoot until you see the whites of their eyes."

Lawrence should have been court-martialed, not martyrized. When he lost that battle, a battle he never should have fought, he lost almost one quarter of the active U.S. Navy. But Great Britain had hundreds of warships left.

It was good for public vanity, this series of sea duels, but that's all it was good for.

The Americans found this draught heady, but the British thought it as black and bitter as gall. There was a great deal of mouthing in British naval circles to the effect that this *couldn't* be true, that there must be a *trick* somewhere. Such fevered talk about "unfair tactics," about the American "disguised ships-of-the-line," must have caused many a Yankee to chuckle. U.S. frigates were better frigates, by and large, than the British ones; but they were frigates all the same. They had more guns—the British naval captains for years had been contending that American frigates were *overgunned,* that they would not stand up under battle conditions—and they had more men. A sloop-of-war, whether ship, brig, or schooner, was a vessel with one gun deck; a frigate, always ship-rigged, had two gun decks; a ship of the line had three or more. That's all there was to it.

Equally absurd was the wail that the Americans were winning because their ships were manned by deserters from the British Navy. To this the wry answer was made that in view of the vast numbers of Americans impressed into the British Navy it could well be asserted that *Guerriere* had lost because she was filled with Americans who would not fight against their own country, while *Constitution* won because she was full of Englishmen who would.

But the British are not always fools, and not for long. Even before the spluttering had subsided there were hard-headed men in the admiralty working on this problem of U.S. naval superiority. Certainly there was a reason for it, probably many reasons, but they did not include treason or cowardice or hidden gun decks. Perhaps British warships should be more heavily manned, even if that meant fewer of them. Perhaps there should be better pay and less brutal punishments, as in the U.S. Navy (the cat-o'-nine-tails was used on American warships, but not often, and thirty lashes was the limit, seldom imposed). It could be that a more stringent system of inspection, especially the inspection of timbers, might be a part of the answer; for didn't some of the survivors of *Guerriere* report that many guns, on recoil, yanked their bolts right out of rotten wood? A heavy cannon broken loose from its fastenings in action was likely to prove an ugly customer in a seaway. There had been other complaints of this kind.

Also, this one-Englishman-is-worth-two-of-anybody-else attitude must end. That was an order. Any British naval captain, unless cornered, who tangled with a vessel demonstrably stronger than his own, win, lose, or draw, was to be cashiered. They'd go out not alone now, but in twos. There would be no more student duels on the high seas.

America cheered itself hoarse at Isaac Hull wherever he appeared. Even news of the fall of Detroit could not dim his splendor, up there beside John Paul Jones; for though Commodore Hull was a nephew of General Hull, who must have been a traitor, and though there were some who whispered that treason runs in families, the man in the street or the field failed to see any connection.

The Navy Department already had made out an order appointing Bainbridge, Hull's superior, to command of *Constitution:* this had been done before Hull sailed from Boston, but it did not reach him in time to stop him. Hull might have embarrassed Washington if he squawked, now that he was an idol, but he was gracious about it, accepting a dull post as chief of naval defenses of the New York City area. He did go to Washington, to get his orders in person, and there, as everywhere, he was made much of, especially by Congressmen. Congress, caught up in the prevailing stir, passed some highly unRepublican appropriations, authorizing the construction of six large frigates and four ships of the line.

It was too late. Not one of those vessels ever got into action. Even if they had, the British Navy was growing much faster. In the first year of this war Great Britain (she laid down even more) *launched* thirteen 74's, one 40-gun frigate, five 38's, fifteen 18-gun sloops, ten 12's, and five smaller war vessels—in itself a fleet far larger than the entire U.S. Navy.

The British were unaccountably slow about applying blockade pressure to America. Not until May 26, 1813, did Admiral Warren at Bermuda issue a proclamation that locked shut the Gulf and Atlantic seaports of America excepting those in New England, and it was December 2 of that year before this was amended to take in Long Island Sound and thus shut off New York City's sneak entry past Montauk. But if it was slow to come, the blockade was steady, it was sure.

Facts are facts, no matter how many flags may flap. In a little while, after that blazing start, the U.S. Navy, gallant though it undoubtedly had been, consisted of a few frigates and sloops of war (the gunboats need not be counted) huddled in remote coves or far upriver, afraid to come out in the open, useless, expensive to maintain, bad for morale, no longer even a threat.

It was bound to be that way. After November 1, 1814, while

an invincible armada was being assembled at the western tip of Jamaica, the United States government did not have a single ship at sea.

Chapter 13

TUT-TUTTERS, POOH-POOHERS of the Great Man theory of history would have had a hard time explaining why the United States was in such a welter of disorganization in the years 1813 and 1814. Nothing was where it should be, while nobody seemed sure of what he was doing. Enlistments were a dribble.[18] Over the greater part of the country times were hard, prices high, money pitifully short, the exception being New England, where, in part because the British blockade had not yet been extended there, in part because of unashamed transborder trade,[19] prosperity reigned; yet it was an uneasy prosperity, and New England stayed bitterly opposed to Jimmy Madison's War, and consented to invest but precious little of its new gold in U.S. government bonds, though willing enough to grab British government bills-of-exchange, which were bought up by the thousands in Boston at 20 to 22 per cent discount. The country skittered along the narrow edge of bankruptcy. The steamboat still was a freak, an experiment, and there never had been much highway travel, so that now, with the coasting trade cut off, one part of what Jefferson had fondly hoped would prove a self-contained country couldn't give the other parts the things they needed. Sugar sold for $9 a hundredweight in New Orleans, but it fetched $40 in New York and Philadelphia. Flour was $3.50 a barrel in Richmond, $17 in Boston.

The Navy of necessity had ceased to shine. The Army struggled on, not with glory, its chief asset the fact that the disorganization in Canada was, if possible, even greater. For Canada, which *had* thrown up an inspired leader early in the war, had lost him again. Brigadier Brock, a whirlwind, as a reward for his capture of Detroit had been made major general and knight of the Bath, but only a few days after this news was received in Canada—he had not been given a chance to get used to being called "Sir Isaac"—he was killed in action at Queenston. This was the most telling thing that had happened to the U.S. arms, so far.

The sage of Monticello might have been expected to step forward, as great heroes traditionally do in the hour of high crisis, but he was too old for that, or thought he was. Moreover, Jefferson never had been a "strong" man, in the political sense. His talents, though they were recognized—for indeed they were felt—were not everywhere admired. It is to be doubted that he could have done much for his protégé, Madison, even if he wished to. An anti-imperialist who when in office had made the biggest national real estate purchase in history, the man who skimped Army and Navy alike of the funds with which to prepare for conflict, and whose gunboats already were a laughing-stock, at first he had been somewhat smug about this affair. "Upon the whole," he wrote a friend ten days after the declaration, "I have known no war entered upon under more favorable auspices." This attitude had changed, perforce. His prediction of the fall of Canada too, though by no means the only one, was remembered.

It was impossible even for the men who owed Madison their jobs to whip up any enthusiasm about the President. Madison did his best. On the day he signed the war proclamation he had put a cockade into his hat and made the rounds of government offices, State, War, and Navy, giving cheerful, informal little talks, an undignified display that must have pained his reticent soul—and that brought only headshakes. His prose style remained clear, mellifluous. He had recently been reelected. But—would the country stay in existence long enough for him to serve out that second term? There were many who doubted it.

James Monroe had the "strong man" temperament. He was impatient, efficient, a driver, not perhaps the military genius he seemed to suppose himself but no fool either. But Monroe was not close to the man who was nominally his chief. He was in the Cabinet not because Madison sought his advice but because Madison thought that he needed his name. And with his earlier attempt to get things done by holding down two posts at the same time Monroe had brought about a protest so shrill that even he, though an impetuous man, would pause a long while before trying anything like that again.

Who else was there?

Certainly not one of the surviving Federalists. Even though they were clamoring these days for states' rights, even though they decried the Louisiana Purchase and called for more warships, they were Federalists all the same. There might be persons of great ability among them, but as a political group they were doomed to slow extinction; and everybody knew this.

Clay? His very brilliance made men shy away from him, as did his too-obvious yearning for the Presidency, not to mention that stiletto, his wit. As much as any one man—for had he not been the most vociferous of the War Hawks?—he was responsible for this mess. He was rather a gleaming star than a sun by which to see one's way.

Albert Gallatin? But no Secretary of the Treasury is ever likely to be popular. Gallatin was a man of great personal charm, aristocratic, dark-complexioned, with fine hazel eyes, and admittedly he was a wizard with figures; but he had a great many enemies, for there were folks who thought that he was *too* clever, *too* smooth, and also, though he had lived for many years in the land of his choice, he had been born abroad, in Switzerland, so that he was not a "true American."

Calhoun? Much too standoffish. He might have had a fine intellect, but he lacked warmth.

Daniel Webster, a bulky, swarthy young man with high cheekbones, coarse black hair, and eyes as dark as anthracite, had come to Congress from New England, though he was no Federalist. But he thought too highly of himself, and let this show. He was a great orator, true; but in manner he was haughty, cold, overbearing.

John Quincy Adams was in Russia; or rather, he had been in Russia, as a singularly successful ambassador, until recently, and he was still abroad.

From the beginning of this war there had been moves to stop it. The British representative in Washington at the time offered to go right back to London with any plan President Madison might propose, himself proposing that there should at least be a suspension of hostilities (which had not even begun yet) until the news could reach England. He was refused, but politely refused; and orders to seek mediation had gone out together with the declaration of war itself to every American ambassador. Jonathan Russell, the U.S. chargé d'affaires in London, acting head of the embassy, had immediately called upon Castlereagh for an armistice. Castlereagh wouldn't listen: he said that Russell did not have the authority to treat. Russell had acted on his own that time, but soon he received orders to reach any informal truce agreement he thought best, and he tried again—and again was turned down. He quit London in a huff, for he was a touchy man, leaving R. J. Beasley, agent for prisoners of war, the highest ranking U.S. representative there.

Britain herself, however, sincerely wanted peace across the Atlantic, and when Admiral Sir John Borlase Warren was sent over to take charge of the naval district that included all the U.S. coast, he carried with him instructions to treat for peace. September 30 of that first year, 1812, he had written to Monroe, the Secretary of State, but this correspondence, though amicable, was unfruitful, for Monroe would not even start to dicker unless England first foreswore impressment, and this Sir John had no authority to do.

Sir George Prevost, governor general of Canada, also very early in the war had communicated by means of a colonel and a flag of truce with Henry Dearborn, commanding the U.S. forces in New York State. Prevost proposed a cease-fire, since it was almost certain, he implied, that the two governments would get together. Dearborn—he wasn't doing anything anyway—agreed. But Washington didn't. Dearborn was reprimanded.

On November 4, 1813, Lord Castlereagh had written directly to his opposite number in the U.S.A., Secretary Monroe; but once again, nothing came of it.

Then an offer to mediate appeared from a most unexpected quarter, the Czar of Russia. This was Alexander I, a good-natured, well-meaning, but utterly unpredictable monarch, who out of a clear sky suggested to Ambassador Adams that he himself, his very own imperial majesty, act as a go-between.

John Quincy Adams was an inexorably, remorselessly honest man, rather short and plump, with rheumy eyes, and great learning, opinionated too, the last person in the world the Czar might have been expected to be intimate with (for the Czar actually had discussed underwear with him). Delighted, and without waiting to learn what England might think of this, Adams sat down and wrote to President Madison, who, just as delighted, appointed Gallatin and a Federalist, Senator James A. Bayard of Delaware, to join Adams in St. Petersburg and for God's sake see what they could do. In such a hurry was Madison that he did not even wait for the Senate to confirm these appointments but packed the two men off on the next ship. The Senate subsequently refused to confirm the appointment of Gallatin (ostensibly on the ground that he couldn't be Secretary of the Treasury and peace commissioner at the same time); but this matter in time was straightened out, so that Gallatin could act.

Nevertheless there was one great man who was about to affect the fate of the United States of America, and to bring about an end to the side war. He was a small tubby unpleasant emperor who had been born on an island most Americans never had heard of—and was destined to die on another island of which the same could be said.

So often and so vehemently had President Madison denied the charge that he was overfriendly with France that it was generally believed to be true, at least in Washington. For one thing, it was pointed out that at the time war was declared it was known everywhere that Napoleon, having gathered around him the Grande Armée of more than 400,000 Frenchmen, Poles, Italians, Prussians, Swiss, Dutch, Austrians, and Rhinelanders was about to invade Russia. Napoleon did in fact cross the Russian frontier exactly five days later. War always is an uncertain business, but it was generally believed in this case that Napoleon would win. How could any nation stand before such a horde? And after that—England. It was all but sure. Napoleon Bonaparte would *enjoy* fighting Great Britain, which could not be said of Americans. And if he did the job for us—he who was so superbly fitted for it—then we might not have to do all that work and spend all that money ourselves, and take all that risk.

This was not a very valiant thought, and probably few men gave it utterance; but it was in the minds of many.

It was not to be. The long dark winter closed over the Grande Armée, and it was not until many months later that strange rumors began to float out of that enigmatic Muscovite land. There had been a disaster, an appalling one. The Corsican was back in France, raising yet *another* army. And now, too, England had some allies.

There came news of sundry battles, odd names that meant nothing to most men in America—Lutzen, Bautzen, Dresden. They were very bloody battles, but curiously they did not seem to be decisive, as most of Napoleon's battles until that time had been. The truth became clear, even at such a distance. A tyrant must always climb. Once he stops to rest he falls back. Whenever the Corsican failed to win a victory, in effect and in fact he suffered a defeat. And this was happening over there. His day was gone. His star was setting.

The last day of March the allies marched into Paris. Eleven days later Napoleon Bonaparte without any qualifications abdicated. Of course he wouldn't keep his word; but the victors would arrange for that. The war in Europe was over. The war in America was about to begin.

Great Britain did not even stop to wash. She didn't put her coat back on. She simply rolled up her sleeves a little higher, and she turned, arms akimbo, to confront that pest across the sea.

Now. . . .

Chapter 14

IT IS SAID that America has produced only two beautiful things —the ax handle and the clipper ship.

No one man, nor group of men, "invented" the clipper, which was a development; but that development was fastest and most marked in the United States in the War of 1812. This was because of the privateers.

The issuance of letters of marque was a form of licensed wartime piracy that already in 1812 was looked upon as some-what old-fashioned. After all, if you had a regular navy, then this was the sort of work your regular navy should do; or, if you didn't have a regular navy, you never should declare war. The effectiveness of privateering in the hands of American skippers alarmed and thoroughly shocked the British public. Some such activity they might have expected, but not so much; nor had they dreamt that the Yankee privateers would be so bold.

In the United States the surprise was by no means as pro-nounced. The chance to loot at sea had been anticipated, and as soon as war was declared there was a rush of applications for letters of marque.

The process of getting such papers was simple, and not ex-pensive. First, a vessel—something small but seaworthy, and above all fast—something that had been engaged in the smuggling trade would be best.

Then, a crew. This part too was easy. There were plenty of seasoned salts. The prewar embargo had caused many hands to be laid off, while the Navy's enlistment terms were expiring, and most of the mariners were only too eager to sign aboard of a privateer and perhaps to win riches. If they too had been smugglers before the war, so much the better. Smugglers knew how to sneak in and out, and how to run.

The crews were large, much larger than the vessel would ordinarily call for; and if he couldn't bully a freighter by the sight of his guns, the privateer, who never wished to fight, at least could threaten a big boarding party. The second reason was the need of prize crews, to take the better vessels to American ports.

Then, armament and supplies. The provisions did not need to be bulky, for the privateer was a hit-and-run operator who never held the seas for a long while on any one cruise. The guns were different. In the first place, these were sometimes hard to buy, so great was the demand. In the second place, if a privateer did not have enough guns he might be beaten off by an armed merchantman, whereas if he had too many guns he might be overweighted and in a chase might have to jettison some—or all. If he could sail into the wind, or even if his vessel was running before a wind that was light, the average American privateer could walk away from any enemy; but if he was forced by circumstances to run before a strong wind and if the vessel that pursued him was large, he could be caught; and it was then that, in order to lighten his craft, he would start tossing overside his cannons—sometimes to no avail.

In the early weeks of the war, for example, while she was making the southerly course that would lead her spang into *Guerrière*, the *Constitution* sighted a vessel and made after it with all canvas set. The other was a privateer out of Boston, and supposed that he was being chased by a British frigate—for what would any such American ship be doing in those waters? It was not the custom to show national colors before speaking, and by the time the privateer learned his mistake he had dropped twelve of his fourteen guns to the bottom, after which there was nothing for him to do but go back to Boston for more.

Of the three kinds of cannons, the columbiad was not used on privateers. The long gun was the most impressive, the most intimidating, the most accurate too, but also the heaviest, and by far. Warships generally used long guns for their far-reaching fights and as bow-chasers; but the privateer never fought at long range and assumed that he could overhaul anything on the sea without resort to bow-chasers. So the privateer—though he took what he could get—preferred the carronade. This was a squat black ugly cannon that wouldn't carry far but could throw a ball very hard when in close, and so was ideally suited for broadside work. The carronade was not nearly as heavy as the long gun, nor did it use as much powder. And it didn't cost anywhere near as much.

The vessel had to be bonded with the government for its full value, this being a precaution against property claims in the event of piracy.

And finally—though this may well have been the first arrangement made—there were the articles of agreement under which the privateer would operate. These were somewhat like the articles under which so many American fishing crews worked. The venture—that is to say, the hoped-for prize money —was divided into "lays," usually sixty-four in number; and "the ship and her owners," who almost invariably included the master, were given half of these, the other half being split among the crew according to a complicated sliding scale which took into account death and wounds and often even contained the proviso that "if any man coward" he should lose entirely his lay or lays. The most important clause, and the one most reminiscent of the Grand Banks contracts, was the "no-fish-no-pay" clause. Privateering was a gamble, and like every gamble it glittered. People talked of the successes; and the failures were forgotten. For every man who made a fortune at privateering, many, many came back penniless. And many others rotted in English jails. Privateers were not hanged, like pirates. Though resented, they were accepted as a legal nuisance. But when they were taken prisoner they were not ordinarily pampered.

The last of the French West Indies had been conquered by Britain, which meant that the few French privateers still at large were deprived of bases. Spanish privateers no longer were to be feared, since Spain and England, like Spain and Portugal, now were allies. A large number of British warships, then, would have been released from the onerous time-consuming convoy duty—had it not been for the United States.

The earliest American privateers in the War of 1812 were quick to take advantage of this. They were small craft, some with only one or two guns, only twenty-five or thirty men, pilot boats in many cases; and they swarmed south like buzzards on the scent of carrion. The pickings were fine, for a little while. But it did not take long to stamp out these scavengers.

This resulted in a new type of privateer, a larger vessel built especially for that business. These, though no pilot boats, still were small; but they were heavily sparred, and each carried a crew of 100 or more. Some were ships, some brigs, or brigantines, or hermaphrodites (brig-schooners), or even, from northern ports, snows; but the favored type, and the most characteristically American, was the schooner.

Built in a rush, few had the decorations dear to mariners' hearts—figureheads, spiral moldings, raised trim, carvings, gilded and painted transoms, headrails; yet by general agreement, even the agreement of British naval historians who hated Yankees, such as James, these vessels were the most beautiful things afloat. Their raked masts, their immense spread of canvas, and low thin sharp bows lent them an appearance of almost incredible grace. And they could live up to this! Not only were they fast, they were dexterous. Seemingly cornered, they could—and again and again did—spin around in the twinkling of an eye and make off on some tack that no other vessel in the world could have taken. When they did manage to capture one, the British would use it as a dispatch boat; but the British never could sail them as the Americans had: their yards did something to the hull and running gear that slowed them, and British skippers wouldn't dare to crack on that much canvas.

They were the wonder of the world, those early clippers; but if they were lovely to look at they were mighty uncomfortable to live in, for they rolled a great deal, having such scant beam and so much canvas, while their sharp bows and low freeboard made for a cramped wet forecastle and a deck that was often awash. No matter. The men who worked them were looking for money, not ease.

There were many reasons why the privateers appeared to be everywhere while the U.S. Navy very soon was bottled up in a few ports. So long as he was at sea each privateering skipper was a law unto himself. He had no assigned duties, no prescribed route. He took what he could get and ran away from whatever he didn't like the looks of. With no department behind him, and not hampered by regulations, he could duck into any port for the hour open and dicker for supplies: he might be fleeced, but he'd get the supplies and be gone from that place before pursuers could close in, a course impossible for the captain of a legitimate warship. The privateer was not concerned with over-all strategy. He was not answerable to faraway admirals and boards of inquiry that might dictate and ruin his future, but only to fellow investors, whose interests were similar to his own. He was not expected to fight, for the honor of the service, any encountered vessel anywhere near his size; on the contrary, he would refuse a brush unless his own superiority was certain. Most important of all, he was—as he could afford to be—unaccountable in his movements. The British Navy had known all about the U.S. Navy before war was declared. Except the cases of a few slipaways early in the conflict, the British knew where to look and what to look for. Their first task was to track down every Yankee warship, no matter where, and either sink it or chase it into a bag—a bag that would henceforth be watched like a mousehole. True, an *Essex* could play hob with official plans; but sooner or later, inevitably, she would be caught. It was not so with the privateers.

The privateers grew bolder with each passing month, and so far from confining themselves to the West Indies they approached the very doorstep of Great Britain itself, poking into the all-but-sacred English Channel, the Narrow Seas. It was maddening.

Some of these marine mosquitoes even had mocking names —*Black Joke, Teazer, Turn Over, Right of Search, Orders in Council.* (That last, a topsail schooner carrying sixteen carronades and a crew of 120, out of New York, had been sensationally lucky until three small British warships forced her under the guns of a 74—and she lost everything.) The well-named brigs, *Scourge* of New York and *Rattlesnake* of Philadelphia, made forty-odd prizes between them, all close to the islands, which cost English merchants and shipowners about $2 million. *True-Blooded Yankee* when she needed firewood took temporary possession of an island off the coast of Ireland and later of a Scottish town. *Boxer, Prince de Neufchatel, Comet, Herald* of Salem, *Swift*—they were positively insolent the way they allowed warships to get near them. Yet two-day chases were not uncommon, and there were some of five or six days, even one on record that lasted eleven days: *it* ended in a capture, the overstrained privateer having lost some of her sail. Thomas Boyle, a quiet unassuming man, of whom such a prank was not to be expected, from the cabin of his dreaded 16-gun schooner *Chasseur*, Baltimore, sent, by a ransomed captive, a "Proclamation" which he said he hoped would be posted at Lloyd's. In this Captain Boyle pointed to the British Navy's habit of declaring paper blockades, and then said that in this same spirit (but it was all put down polysyllabically and with an exceedingly straight face) he found himself called upon to "declare all the ports, harbors, bays, creeks, rivers, inlets, islands, and seacoast of the United Kingdom of Great Britain and Ireland in a state of strict and rigorous blockade."

The cheek of the man!

Insurance rates soared. Just to cross the Irish Channel cost a 13 per cent premium, while the price elsewhere was more than twice as high as it had been even during the war with France.

Outraged, the mercantile moguls, the very ones who in England had done the most to bring it about, were clamoring for the end of this war. The London *Times* might aver that the hour had come to administer some "merited chastisement" upon the United States of America; but the money men, squealing in pain, cried to hell with revenge, as previously they had cried to hell with glory.

Yet, as was the case with the frigate duels in the early part of the war, it was not as bright as it immediately looked.

At no time were there fifty American privateers cruising, and seldom if ever did any two of them work together, even for a little while. The Navy could have done a better job with fewer raiders, if after Hull's victory an exultant Congress, instead of the frigates and ships of the line that never were completed, had authorized a fleet of war sloops, which could have been built in less than one quarter of the time. The Navy, when it captured a vessel it couldn't conveniently take in, burned that vessel rather than let the enemy have it back. The privateers too sometimes did this, or sometimes managed to ransom the vessel, but often, especially if it was a good craft, in itself of value, they stripped it and sent it for a home port under a prize crew. Time after time this prize, lacking the speed of its captor, would be picked up by the British Navy. There were 515 registered U.S. privateers in this second war with England—150 from Massachusetts, 112 from Maryland, 102 from New York, 31 from Pennsylvania, 16 from New Hampshire, 15 from Maine (really a part of Massachusetts then), 11 from Connecticut, 9 from Virginia, 7 from Louisiana, 7 from Georgia, and 55 from ports not designated [20]—and they took a total of 1,345 prizes, at least that they reported. Of these it has been reckoned that about half were sent to American ports, and that about half of *those,* or a quarter of the whole, were recaptured before they could get to the United States. At a conservative estimate that meant at least 6,500 seamen who sat out the war in British jails—crack sailors, all of them, the best in the business, men who except for the privateering system would have gone into the U.S. Navy, which, as it was, was manned largely by foreigners.

Joshua Barney of Baltimore, a former naval officer, had a fling at privateering, early in the war. He was phenomenally successful, one of the pointed-ats, for with *Rossie* he took fifteen prizes in forty-five days, and got them all back. But he said he wouldn't do it again, though he was made some fancy offers. By the time the split with the government had been paid, together with all the other charges—for seized goods were dutiable—it just wasn't worth it. Joshua Barney re-enlisted in the Navy.

As early as November in the first year of the war the owners of twenty-four New York privateering vessels petitioned Congress for relief. They were starving, they said. At that time Congress, on the advice of the Secretary of the Treasury, Gallatin, refused; but the following year, in August—Gallatin meanwhile having gone to Europe as a peace commissioner— Congress reduced by one-third the duties on prize goods, offered a bounty of $25 a prisoner brought in by privateers, and authorized the Secretary of the Navy to pension wounded privateersmen. After that the business picked up a little—but only a little.

Chapter 15

THE WAR WAS waxing nasty. There was no more talk of cease-fires. It was with a snarl, not a smile, that England addressed herself at last to this pesky conflict in the outlands.

After Van Rensselaer's defeat at Queenston the Yankee prisoners were taken to Quebec, where they were intensively and individually questioned, twenty-three of them being weeded out as British born—and hence, in British eyes, British. These twenty-three were sent to England on charges of having borne arms against their own country. It was an odds-on bet that they would be hanged.

Armstrong, the American Secretary of War, when he heard of this, ordered that twenty-three English prisoners should be picked by lot from those taken in the same battle and segregated as hostages. England responded by segregating as hostages *twice* that number, or forty-six, of her prisoners, besides the original twenty-three.

It went no further, possibly because neither army, after all, had many prisoners to bargain with, while naval prisoners, in this connection, didn't count.

A peppery small Scot, Admiral Sir George Cockburn, ranged up and down the coasts of Maryland and Virginia, landing any place he pleased, paying for whatever he took provided there was no show of resistance, but burning and looting unmercifully when there was. Most of these operations were on a small scale, but when Cockburn approached Norfolk it was at the head of the largest fleet the British yet had assembled on the west side of the sea—eight ships of the line, twelve frigates, and many smaller craft, most of which a little later were to be sent to Negril Bay.

Norfolk he found too tough a nut to crack, so he went across the bay to Hampton, a place of no military importance. Hampton's handful of militiamen scurried, and the town was taken. It quaked, to be sure, for Cockburn was no Bayard, *sans peur et sans reproche,* and he had made his methods only too well known. The night passed quietly; but the next morning all hell broke loose. Whether it was deliberate, or because of some sudden whim, never will be known; but it is certain at least that the officers didn't do much, when they did anything at all, to stop it. In the medieval sense, the town was turned over to the troops. Soldiery went wild, roaming the streets, stripping houses. One old man, bedridden, was murdered in cold blood, and his wife was badly slashed when she tried to protect him. Several women were mass-raped.

The effect seared. British morale, in the field, was crippled, especially among the officers, who were asking one another if they really were soldiers or just marauders. There were recriminations within their own ranks; and the official, and prompt United States protest was fervent. The British excused the looting and burnings on the ground of resistance, but for the rapine they found a scapegoat. This was a comparatively small body of French prisoners of war, who, bored with life behind bars, had volunteered to serve in a green-coated outfit called the Chasseurs Britanniques. They were but a handful of the occupying force at Hampton, but they were the only ones guilty, their superiors said, of rape. Nobody believed this, even after the Chasseurs Britanniques had been dismissed from the service. (They hadn't been very efficient anyway, and the British no longer needed soldiers.)

But the memory of Hampton was to rankle for a long while.

Neither had the Canadians forgotten York (Toronto), and there were sundry other over-the-border outrages, notably a raid on Long Point, Lake Erie, in which some mills and houses were burned by irresponsible Yankees. Most of these were unauthorized, and in some cases the guilty parties were punished; but in wartime, denials go for nothing.

There was an interlude of heroism. Oliver Hazard Perry had been in the Navy since the age of fifteen, and had seen no action at all but a great deal of hard service, when, a lieutenant at twenty-seven, he was in charge of a squadron of those inglorious gunboats off Newport, Rhode Island. There Perry got orders to go to Lake Erie and take charge of the work of building a fleet. At Presque'ile (Erie, Pa.) he performed wonders. There were many handicaps: Presque'ile was in the wilderness and everything had to be hauled there, the nearest supply base being Pittsburgh, four days' hard pull; Perry's men for the most part were raw, sloppy; he himself suffered from a bilious fever that infested the camp; his opposite number, Captain Robert H. Barclay, R.N., building a similar fleet at

Malden, on the Detroit River, at thirty-two had seen much more action than Perry, having, for one thing, lost an arm at Trafalgar; while Perry's superior, Commodore Chauncey, U.S.N., (though the same thing could be said of Barclay's superior, Yeo) kept most of the best seamen, craftsmen, and materials on Lake Ontario. Nevertheless, when Perry at last sailed forth with his green vessels—this was September 10, 1813 —he was ready to fight.

The fleets were evenly matched. The battle was fierce. The United States victory was complete.

It would no longer be possible for the British even to hope to send supplies to Detroit or to Malden, which in consequence they couldn't hold. Their Indian allies in those parts, unfed, would vanish.

Perry's own flagship, a 17-gun brig, was called *Lawrence*, after the man who had lost *Chesapeake* in a frigate duel, and before the battle Perry had caused to be made a huge square blue muslin flag on which were stitched in letters of white Lawrence's dying words: "Don't give up the ship." This Perry displayed prominently, just before coming to grips with the British. Yet he himself was to give his nation a more inspiring and much less negative slogan when, after the action, he reported to General Harrison: "We have met the enemy, and they are ours."

It helped, but it could hardly be enough. After the splatter of battles around Leipzig, October 16, 17 and 18 of that year 1813, when it became clear that Boney's number was up, the British began to extend and to tighten their blockade, and driblets of infantry came over to Canada, so that as the summer of '14 approached, the reports could be positively verified that the British were engaged in sending 16,000 veterans. All the rallying cries in the world wouldn't prevail against such a force. The United States might again, and did again, invade small sections of Upper Canada; but the Niagara region, the St. Lawrence region, were lost. Any *real* invasion, after this, would be in a southerly direction, from Canada into the United States.

President Madison on the last day of the March 1813 session of Congress had signed the foreign seamen act, providing that after the war *all* aliens, from whatever country they came, would be prohibited from acting as sailors aboard United States public *or* private vessels. It was an unashamed plea for peace; but it stirred little interest in England; and when the delegates were sent to St. Petersburg it was with instructions—also sent to John Quincy Adams, who was already there and was to be a third delegate—that the renunciation of the principle of impressment was a *sine qua non*. They themselves, the delegates, Gallatin and Senator Bayard, believed that for this reason the discussion probably never would start.

They had a weary time of it in Russia, those delegates. The czar was in the field with his armies, and nothing could be done until he returned. They didn't get along well with Adams, who was cantankerous at best and hardly a man for working in harness. They learned to their dismay that the Senate back home had refused to confirm the appointment of Gallatin, and later, with even greater dismay, they learned that the British absolutely, if tactfully, refused to accept the mediation of the Emperor Alexander.

Great Britain did say, however, that she'd be willing to treat directly with the United States, if the U.S. delegates would go to Ghent, say, or to Gothenburg, Sweden, or to Amsterdam, or, better still, come to London. That last honor (meanwhile the U.S. Senate had reversed itself, confirming Gallatin's appointment) they refused, formally; though Bayard and Gallatin did go to the English capital of their own accord, as private tourists, at the invitation of Alexander Baring, the banker. Two others had been appointed to this commission, one of them Jonathan Russell, until lately U.S. chargé d'affaires at London, who had recently been named minister to Sweden and was at Stockholm now, and the other the ebullient, hard-drinking Henry Clay, who had resigned as Speaker of the House.

By this time it was winter, the winter of 1813-14, the worst, as of weather, in the history of Europe. Communications being what they weren't, it took a long while for these various delegates to get together, having settled upon a place, Ghent; and there they had to wait a long while, again, for the English delegates to be appointed and to appear. The English delegates were three: Lord Gambier, a retired naval personage, red-faced, hot-tempered, not too intelligent, a man who, as Gallatin noted in his diary, was like "a firecracker which would never go off but was always spluttering"; Dr. William Adams, an ill-natured, rather coarse expert in maritime law; and Henry Goulburn, a young and very earnest man. Here was a much weaker delegation than that of the United States. This was but natural. Ghent was little more than a British outpost, quartered by British troops, so that the delegates from London might almost as well have been home. It took them about ten days to report to their superiors in the Foreign Office, and to get an answer. It would have taken the United States delegation more than two months to do that. The British commissioners were little more than exalted errand boys, at that distance; and it didn't really matter if they were stupid. The Foreign Office was more interested just then in a really big peace conference that was shaping up in Vienna.

The first meeting at Ghent was held August 8, 1814. It was stiff, and didn't get far. There were several other sessions that month. Nothing much was accomplished. The British were not authorized to accept a renunciation of impressment as a *sine qua non,* and in their turn they demanded several such—Yankee fishing rights on the Banks, agreed to in the treaty of 1783, were to end; a cession to Great Britain, for purposes of easier communication, of various tracts in Maine, amounting to 233,000,000 acres, worth about $5 million; the Mississippi to be opened to British traffic, free, and access to its upper waters guaranteed; an Indian buffer state to be set up under British auspices, and to remain under British control, which would include about one-third of Ohio, two-thirds of Indiana, and almost all of what is now Illinois, Wisconsin, and Michigan.

This was preposterous.

The American delegates sighed. They knew that their government, howsoever desperate, would never—*could* never—consent to such terms. But it would take time to confirm this. So they sent the message; and then they sat down, yet again, to wait.

Chapter 16

"YOU ARE HEREBY required and directed to destroy and lay waste such towns and districts upon the coast as you may find assailable . . . and you will spare merely the lives of unarmed inhabitants," Vice Admiral the Honorable Sir Alexander Cochrane, K.B., at Bermuda, July 18, 1814, wrote in an order to all of those under his command—that is, all the British Navy forces in America: Cochrane lately had replaced Sir John Borlase Warren.

Cochrane is not to be confused with that other short-tempered Scottish knight-admiral, Cockburn, though there are many points of resemblance. Cochrane, who was a little older, fifty-five, and ranked higher, was a brother of the 9th earl of Dundonald. Another brother, Charles, had been killed at Yorktown. Cochrane hated Yankees, and he did not mind saying so. His ostensible reason for issuing this get-harsh order was a message from the governor-general of Canada, Sir George Prevost, who informed him of the Long Point raid, and, rather unaccountably (since Prevost was a major general in the Army), suggested that the Navy do something in the way of reprisals. Cochrane didn't have to be asked a thing like that twice; yet it is safe to assume that the governor-general's letter was but a convenient pretext, and that Cochrane would have issued that order, or something like it, anyway.

Still another Scot, Major General Robert Ross, had recently

arrived with a brigade of 2,300 Peninsular veterans, to which was added, in Bermuda, a battalion, bringing the total number of effectives under Ross to about 3,400.[21] Ross had orders to scourge the American coast as an independent military commander working in co-operation with Admiral Cochrane. In the orders of both men this stroke-to-come was somewhat euphemistically set down as a "diversion," to take pressure off Canada; but the implication that it should not be done in a mollycoddling way was clear; and these were the men to do it, these two. The decision as to where the first blow should fall was left to Admiral Cochrane, and he agreed that Admiral Cockburn (who was still on the party) had been right, and that Chesapeake Bay was best suited for their predatory purposes— at first. Cochrane and Ross, then, sailed from Bermuda August 3. Their faces were grim.

Prevost too went about his work grimly, in Canada, though he might well have smiled. True, the Yankees still held the Lakes, so that he had lost Detroit and the greater part of his Indian allies; and it was true too that the latest battles, border affairs, but very bloody, Chippewa and Lundy's Lane, had gone the Yankee way, though they had settled nothing; but it was also true that the promised reinforcements, veterans, were pouring in, so that he had a huge advantage over his neighbors to the south. He could offset Perry's victory by an invasion of the Hudson River valley, for which he had the men, as he had the guns. Everything, now, depended upon control of Lake Champlain, that lovely inland sea on the shores of which Captain Thomas Macdonough, U.S.N., and Captain George Downie, R.N., were engaged in a frantic fleet-building race, very much as Barclay and Perry had been a little while ago at opposite ends of Lake Erie.

Part of Prevost's perturbation might have been due to a well-backed rumor that the Duke of Wellington had been sounded out about taking command in Canada, and had replied that he would do so if ordered, of course, but hoped he wouldn't be ordered. The Iron Duke gave three reasons:

1. Because of his prestige as the conqueror of Boney, he

might be of more use to his country in Paris or Vienna, where the peace of Europe was being made.

2. There could be no final military ascendancy in Canada until command of the Great Lakes was assured, and just now the United States had this: in other words, the problem was a naval one, and he, the Duke, was not a naval man.

3. Would not this assignment look to the rest of the world like a last resort, a sign of weakness, when in fact Great Britain was anything *but* weak?

Prevost had no cause for complaint. When he crossed the border, September 3, it was at the head of the biggest force that ever had invaded the United States. Not Amherst nor Guy Carleton, not Lord Cornwallis nor yet Gentleman Johnny Burgoyne led such a mighty army. There were six major generals, a score of brigadiers, and at least 11,000 crack infantrymen, plus the artillery, in itself greatly superior to anything the Yankees could show.

Everything depended upon the navies, the fleets. These were about the same size and were manned by the same number of men, 800. As on Lake Erie, they had been built to fight the same battle—just one. The British had more guns, but the American guns, up close, could throw a greater weight of metal. So Macdonough was determined that the fight should *be* up close. He posted himself in Plattsburg Bay and would not go out into the lake proper, as Downie wished him to do. Among the invading force the Navy and the Army had been squabbling even more shrilly than was usual, and Downie, who thought that he was being pushed, and resented it, might have been goaded by time to go into the bay. Anyway, and for whatever reason—nobody ever will know, for Downie was killed in this action, and his papers, subsequently, were destroyed by accident—he did go in.

It was a beautiful September Sunday morning, the leaves of the trees already beginning to change, the shores of Plattsburg Bay black with spectators—for surely this would be a spectacle.

With the two sides so nearly even, preparation counted more than ever. Macdonough had made his plans well, and he fought on his own terms. His vessels were anchored, and there were springs on those anchors—that is, there were several lines from each anchor to its ship, so that the ship could be worn around to better her firing position. Because of this, Macdonough spread no canvas and he was able to lower and stow away his lighter spars, thus cutting the danger of splinters. The British, on the other hand, were obliged to approach under sail. There simply wasn't enough sea room for them even to try to turn Macdonough's flanks, nor could they stay at a distance and batter him with long-range guns. In truth, there was to be no maneuvering in this battle, and not even a threat of boarding. The two sides simply got close together and slugged it out.

Downie was killed very early, in the first few minutes of fighting [22], a great stroke of luck for the Americans. Many, many others were killed. All of the vessels, from the mighty British frigate *Confiance* to the tiniest gunboat, were badly mauled. The decks ran with blood. The British fought on for more than an hour and a half, and at the time they struck—every one of them—there was scarcely a stick standing on either side. A salt who had been there remarked that Trafalgar was "a fleabite to this," the last naval engagement between English-speaking peoples.

The win was emphatic, complete. It almost seemed a miracle, so much had hung upon it.

"The Almighty has been pleased to grant us a signal victory," reported Macdonough, who was a very religious young man and came from New Castle, Delaware. Oddly, this explanation brought about a great deal of anger among the English, who themselves had been known to attribute success to supernatural influence; but it seemed perfectly clear to the compatriots of Thomas Macdonough.

The effect of the battle of Lake Champlain upon Sir George Prevost was extraordinary. He didn't do any shooting, or even any further scouting. He simply turned around and went back to Canada.

Here was a great cause for rejoicing south of the border, and a dramatic naval event, but it was hardly a turning point in the war. Indeed, it left everything about where it had been before. Admittedly it did offer a breathing space. There would be no further invasion of the United States *that year*. But—would the United States last until the following spring? And if it did? Prevost's magnificent army, though so badly led the first time, was undiminished: it remained bigger and better equipped than anything that the Yankees could possibly produce. No doubt Prevost would soon be recalled—he was—and a less timorous general sent over. What then?

The blockade was extended to cover all of New England, now that so many more warships were available. Here and there along the coast—as at Stonington, Conn., for example—a British warship or a small fleet of them senselessly if savagely bombarded a town, picking these, it would seem, at random, not trying to occupy them, only using them for target practice. There was no resistance to these atrocities. There couldn't be.

Since the Revolution the British had been worried about the poor land connections between the Nova Scotian peninsula and Quebec—the St. Lawrence was icebound each winter—and it was for this reason that their diplomats at that very time, in Ghent, were demanding so much of Maine. Their military forces at Halifax did more: working with the Royal Navy, they descended upon the Maine coast, occupied all the islands in Passamaquoddy Bay—Moose, Frederick, Dudley, and two small ones—and sailed up the Penobscot and burned *Adams*, the last U.S. frigate to hold the high seas, which had gone there for refitting. Thus they controlled all the Maine coast east of that river, about 100 miles of it—and without firing a shot. They required the inhabitants to take an oath of allegiance to King George, something none of them minded doing.

The head of that expedition, Sir John Coape Sherbrooke, lieutenant-general of Nova Scotia, soon afterward was approached by a representative of the Commonwealth of Massachusetts. What this man offered has never been made public—nor has his name—but it is certain that Sherbrooke was enough impressed to write to his superior, Lord Bathurst, the Foreign

Secretary, a warning that Great Britain might do well to make ready for the formation of a separate state in America, an eastern or northern confederacy.[23] England knew this anyway. The demands of Great Britain had been made public when received in Washington, bringing a howl of rage from the American people, followed by at least as loud a howl from England, where the publication was denounced as improper, unethical, not cricket; but the Federalists of Boston were not fazed,[24] and indeed their secessionist plans were more open than ever, and everybody knew that a New England convention to discuss the subject had been called for Hartford, December 15. Massachusetts, Connecticut, and Rhode Island certainly would be represented at that convention, and probably New Hampshire, and perhaps Vermont as well; but Massachusetts if she had to could make the step alone, for Massachusetts not only was the second most populous state, but she controlled virtually all of the nation's specie, and her militia, as yet untouched, well equipped, well drilled, numbered 70,000 men—more than twice as much as the whole U.S. Army put together. If Massachusetts elected to get out, slamming the door, she could. And it looked as if she would, taking several other states with her. That would be the end of the Union.

Cockburn, Cochrane, and Ross were assailed by no such self-doubts as had plagued the governor-general of Canada. They went about their work fiercely and well.

At their approach, the only water defense in Chesapeake Bay, sixteen gunboats under the command of that erstwhile privateer Joshua Barney, retreated up the Patuxent, where, to prevent them from falling into the hands of a British landing force, Barney had them blown up—though he saved the guns.

That landing force was under General Ross in person. It took its time, meeting not a trace of resistance, and seemingly uncertain for a while whether to pounce upon Baltimore, the more important place, or Washington, which wasn't fortified and which was, after all, the capital. Suddenly it swerved toward Washington.

The city's defense was in the hands of a political appointee, who had done as near to nothing as could be.[25] He mustered his forces now on a slope at Bladensburg, a few miles north and east of the city. They were mostly militia, though there were a few regulars, and Barney had brought along his 400 boatless sailors. It was absurd. With the irritable gesture of a man who in darkness walks into a cobweb, the vanguard of the British routed this mass. A few of the regulars didn't run right away, though neither did they linger. Barney and his sailors fought gallantly, and virtually alone, 400 against 4,000, many of them being bayoneted at their guns. But the rest was—for America—disgrace.

Ross and Cockburn entered Washington the next morning. It was a rather mean hamlet, except for the public buildings, which were splendid. The British burned the public buildings. There was no *general* fire. Everything was deliberately done, on direct orders from the general or the admiral—some of the men were marines. One of the biggest fires of all in Washington that day, however, was that set by the retreating Americans—they burned down the shipyard, a patent military objective. The rest was the work of the invaders. That some of this was saved was thanks not to the British but to a sudden and very violent rainstorm.

Afterward, like guilty boys, as though they feared that some-body was chasing them—they *needn't* have feared that: the al-together unmauled American army was retreating still, the other side of the city—the British went quickly back to their boats; though a frigate did make its way up the Potomac as far as Alexandria, a city it held to ransom, sailing downstream again with a tremendous booty.

The Capitol, like the White House, was in ashes. The President of the United States, a smallish frightened sixty-three-year-old man, was hiding somewhere in the Virginia hills, his Cabinet scattered, out of touch with one another. The original Declaration of Independence, stuffed into a linen bag, had been given refuge for the night in an old barn, the property of one Edgar Patterson, two miles above Chain Bridge. Nobody knew what to expect, or whom to obey. Chaos, it would seem, was just around the corner.

Baltimore had been given a chance to entrench. It too depended largely upon militia, but this time there was a leader, Senator Sam Smith, who meant business, and there were no meddling politicians, as there had been at Bladensburg.

It was a stirring fight, but none too well conducted on the part of the British Navy. Because of vessels sunk across the entrance of the harbor the big warships could not get in close enough even to protect their outflung smaller vessels. The best they could do, while a landing party confronted or was about to confront a well-dug-in protective force, was hammer all night at Fort McHenry, which, it was clear, had to be knocked out first.

Fort McHenry refused to be knocked out. It was strong. Only a handful of its 1,000-men garrison was killed. The fort stood, and with the coming of dawn it was seen that the flag still floated above it, a circumstance that inspired a young Baltimore lawyer, Francis Scott Key, to write some verses, which he fitted to the old London drinking-club song, "To Anacreon in Heaven," and which were to prove very popular.

In a retreat the rear is the post of honor, since it is the place of greatest peril, and it was in the rear that General Ross was as his men backed away from those entrenchments the next morning after the Navy had admitted failure. There he was when an American sniper killed him.

This cast a cat's-paw of gloom upon the raiders, for Ross had been loved, and it did seem a shame that he couldn't have gone down as he himself would have liked, in a real fight, facing the enemy. But spirits soon rose. If some officers did tend to mumble that they were being made to behave like outlaws, for the most part, in both services, hearts were high and voices glad.

They all knew where they were going, after Baltimore. They were going to the rendezvous at Negril Bay. It won't be long now, they told one another. New Orleans will be easy.

Chapter 17

THIS MAN JACKSON was a killer. He was not taken from any pattern, not stamped out by a cookie-cutter. Granted, he was a product of the frontier, lank, hard, unpredictable, edgy, chivalrous to a high degree, the kind of man who didn't just talk about it but actually *liked* to fight; yet by the same token he was an individualist. He had had little training in any skill (if butting, gouging, kicking, shooting, punching, and the swift use of a knife be excepted), but he had his own ideas, and he would stick to them, for he was prodigiously stubborn.

He was tall, thin to the point of emaciation, always in delicate health, and he stood very straight. No beauty, he had light-blue, direct, what-d'ye-want eyes, and turbulent, light-brown hair, a long pale mouth that was like a razor slash, a pump-handle chin. He was proper in the presence of ladies, profane in the presence of men. He preferred the presence of men.

He was a son, the youngest, of Scotch-Irish immigrants who had settled in the back country of North Carolina, near the South Carolina line. His father died before he was born. His mother died of jail fever contracted while nursing prisoners of war in the Revolution, and one of his brothers died in battle in that war, while the other died as a result of disease caught in a foul British prison, a prison to which the boy Andrew also was confined and from which perhaps he never really recovered. He fought his first acknowledged battle at Hanging Rock, August 1, 1780, and no doubt he enjoyed it, though he was only thirteen, for he was to be fighting additional battles for the rest of his life. He was not hit at Hanging Rock, but he did bring out a couple of wounds from that war. A prisoner, the boy was ordered by an English officer to black his, the officer's boots. He refused. The officer drew and slashed down at him, and Andrew raised his arm, which was not enough wholly to shield his head, so that both were cut. He was to flaunt those scars for the rest of his life. He was proud of them. He wouldn't have given them up for all the tea in China—and they didn't hurt him politically, either.

It will be seen that Andrew Jackson had cause to hate the English. He never denied this. Nor was he a forgive-and-forget man. The milk of kindness was not in him.

He was brought up—more or less—by an uncle and aunt. He was a wild lad, though not vicious. He loved gambling, cock-fights, horse races. He went to Charleston for a little while, but decided that city life was not for him, and returned to the backwoods, where he studied law. The requirements were not stringent; and law was the thing to take up if you happened to be penniless, ambitious, and not entirely without letters. There was always a call for lawyers along that disputatious frontier.

In later days, amid the elegances of Washington, D.C., much was to be made of this man's education—or lack thereof. It even came to be said that he was responsible for that most widespread of all Americanisms, O.K., from a habit of passing on papers with a scrawled "Oll Korrect." This is absurd.[26] Andrew Jackson's English was sound, if limited. He was a slap-dash speller, by no means the only one the world knew, but his grammar was fairly good. If in his public pronouncements he sometimes slipped into rant, this was only the instinctive bullying of a backwoodsman. To him, as to the men among whom he grew up, bombast was natural, an accepted form. Andrew Jackson had a high sense of dignity, and when the occasion called for it he could be as circumspect as the next man. Conceivably a part of the popular picture can be accounted for by the General's refusal to use "fancy" language. In his correspondence, and perhaps in his speech, he might toss off some tag like *Carthago delenda est,* a favorite at the time; but these were the commonplaces of political oratory, the rubber stamps of the stump: they meant nothing in themselves. Andrew Jackson never pretended to a knowledge of classical literature. But nobody was in doubt as to what he meant.

Restless, he decided to go farther west and to grow up with the country, and this he did, settling in the village of Nashville, in what was then called the western provinces of North Carolina. He had been a constable and a deputy sheriff, but now truly he was an attorney, and he prospered in a mild way. When the section applied for admission into the Union as a separate state, young Jackson was one of those who helped to draw up its constitution, and he was the first that Tennessee sent to the National House of Representatives in Philadelphia. He was no orator, and did not distinguish himself in Congress, except by the vehemence of his dislike for George Washington, or at least for the fashionable adulation of Washington, who was at that time leaving public life: Andrew Jackson was one of a handful of Congressmen who refused to sign the fulsome salute of departure. Later he was elected to the U.S. Senate, but he never went there much. He couldn't abide the Senate. Too stuffy.

At last, and still in his twenties, he was appointed chief justice of Tennessee's highest court. This suited him, and he held the job for many years; and indeed it was as Judge Jackson rather than as Colonel or General Jackson that his friends and neighbors knew him.

He never was a rich man, but he did well enough in the law, on the bench, and in private investments. The land was growing up, all around him, and like practically every one of his associates and friends he bought in heavily of acreage, making good profits when later settlers came along. He wasn't "smart," but he was there; and everything was going up.

Cash was not always handy, and often he was paid in kind. The kind included slaves. He had a few slaves of his own at The Hermitage, his home near Nashville, and those that he took in payment of legal services he invariably sold through a trader, who shipped them down the river. If Jackson had any feeling about this, one way or the other, he never expressed it.

Before he bought The Hermitage Andrew Jackson as a young

lawyer lived in a boardinghouse in Nashville. The keeper of that boardinghouse had a daughter, and this daughter had a husband, a drinking man, who left her to return to his native Virginia. Soon after this breaking-up, Rachel Robards, *née* Donelson, learned that her husband, as she understood it, had been granted a decree of divorce by the Virginia legislature. In fact all he had been granted was permission to apply for such a decree; and it is amazing that Jackson, even though he might not have been much of a student of law, would not have known this; but amazing or not, it must be believed, for whatever Andrew Jackson might not have been he was honest—he was *fiercely* honest. Anyway, they were married; and it was not until two years later that they learned they had been living in sin. Jackson then arranged to get the divorce, and they were remarried.

Rachel made him a good if unexciting wife. They never had any children of their own, though they adopted no fewer than *eleven*, including, rather unexpectedly—for the Judge like all his neighbors hated Indians [27]—an Indian boy.

Rachel was always somewhat square, and she grew fat, nor was she remarkable for intelligence. But she was a deeply religious woman, and she worshiped Andrew, who for his part adored her.[28]

It was not a time for the pulling of political punches, and his enemies made much of this mistake, sneeringly asserting that Andy Jackson had stolen another man's wife. But they never said this to his face! for he was quick to produce a weapon. He was touchy about almost everything, but he was especially touchy about those two illegitimate years with Rachel.

When "Nolichucky Jack" Sevier, the governor of Tennessee, refused to approve of Andrew Jackson as general of militia, Jackson was furious; and another feud was begun. But it was not until Sevier in a public speech referred to Jackson as a man who had stolen another man's wife, that Jackson really exploded. "Great God, do you mention *her* sacred name?" He challenged. Sevier refused on the ground that his record in the Revolution was sufficient proof of his courage. Jackson threatened to shoot him on sight anyway, and several times he nearly did so, his friends holding him back.

His first duel, oddly enough, had nothing to do with Rachel. It arose from some high words exchanged in court with a lawyer, Colonel Waitsill Avery. That had been in 1795, and a comparatively mild meeting, for they both fired into the air.

His encounter with Charles Dickinson, in 1806, was quite different. They had been squabbling for some time, at long distance, and whenever the quarrel seemed to die (it had started about a race horse) somebody whispered to Jackson that Dickinson had spoken lightly of Rachel. On the other hand, it might be that it was Jackson's enemies rather than his friends who brought about the duel, for Dickinson was known to be the best pistol shot in Tennessee.

Jackson was worried, going to the field of honor with his principal second, General Thomas Overton. Jackson was not worried about his life. He never did that. But he really hated Charles Dickinson, who really hated him: this was not to be any shooting-in-the-air, not a meeting *à plaisance*, but rather a meeting *à outrance*, to the death.

Dickinson was the better shot: Jackson and Overton were agreed on that. The distance was to be not the conventional ten paces but *eight* paces—a pace was assumed to be a long stride, for all practical purposes one yard—and who could miss at twenty-four feet? The first to shoot would kill. Dickinson was known to be a very fast, as also a very accurate, marksman —a man who pointed his pistol as readily as he would point his forefinger in accusation, a *natural*. Overton and Jackson, riding to the field, decided that Jackson's only chance was to accept the first shot, hoping that it would miss, which was unlikely, or that it would not hit a vital spot, which was possible but still unlikely. Then, if Jackson was still alive—and *that* was unlikely too—he would have a clear target.

The day was May 30, and clear. The place was to be on the Kentucky bank of the Red River, just over the Tennessee state line. There was a large crowd.

Dickinson laughed as he strode out. Jackson, clad in a long loose frock coat, looking very old, did not laugh. It can be doubted that Jackson ever *did* laugh.

A tossed coin made Overton the referee, and the distance was measured, the principals placed. It had been agreed that the principals at first should not face one another, but, with their pistols in their hands hung loose, muzzles toward the ground, should face the referee. At a signal they should turn toward one another and fire at will.

Overton stood halfway between the two, but off to one side, out of the expected line of fire.

Pegs had been driven into the earth at each end of the field, to mark the distance. A principal must come up to his peg, as a pugilist to the scratch, and was not allowed to retreat from it.

Overton asked each if he was ready, and received from each the reply, "I am ready, sir."

"You may fire, gentlemen!"

They turned, and Dickinson fired instantly. Jackson, slower, lifted his pistol, but did not otherwise move.

Dickinson could not believe this. He staggered back.

"My God, have I missed?"

General Overton was prompt, and proper: *"Stand to your peg, sir!"*

So Dickinson, that fine handsome foolish hard-drinking young man, stepped forward, and he stood to the peg. But he had to close his eyes. He was human.

Andrew Jackson didn't gloat, but he did take his time. He leveled his pistol carefully, and when he was ready he pulled the trigger.

The striker fell at half-cock.

Under the agreement this was not a shot. And Andrew Jackson was entitled to a shot.

The seconds fussily examined Jackson's pistol, and recocked it. Then they stepped back.

"You may fire."

Dickinson still had his eyes closed. He was probably praying.

Jackson fired.

Dickinson went down, screaming in pain.

When the etiquette-demanded bows had been made, and the departure of the man who survived was assented to by the representatives of the man who hadn't, Andrew Jackson walked off the field with General Thomas Overton. Jackson's step was steady, though he could scarcely stand. He was damned if he would let it be seen that he'd been hit.

The bullet from Dickinson's gun, an ounce-and-a-half slug of lead, had gone through the loose part of Jackson's coat—for Jackson had turned his body inside that coat, as he was entitled to do—and had caught what Dickinson assumed was the place of the heart. But the heart wasn't there. The bullet had entered Jackson's body just outside the ribs on the right side, and it had skittered clear around those ribs, chipping them, under the skin, missing the heart by less than a half-inch, to lodge in the muscles under the left arm. Jackson had blood flowing down his body inside his clothes when he quit the field with that stiff angular gait of his. The blood filled his boots. But he did not waver, knowing that it didn't show. Beyond the limits of the field of honor he fainted; and it took him a long while to recover—he never did recover, really, for he carried that bullet in his body the rest of his life. Well, he had done what he set out to do. He had killed Charles Dickinson.

"I would have fired the same way," he said afterward, solemnly, "if the bullet had gone through my brain."

He believed this—there is no doubt of it. And everybody who knew him believed it.

This, then, was the man who was to keep the British from taking New Orleans—if he could.

Chapter 18

KNIGHTS OF OLD spent more time in bed than on horseback.
This was because they were forever getting their bones broken.
Something like the same situation existed in western Tennessee in the early part of the nineteenth century.

When they came to tell Andrew Jackson, in 1813, that the
Creeks had gone on the warpath and to ask him if he would
take charge of the campaign against them, they found him flat
on his back, weak and pale and in great pain from a bullet
wound in the left shoulder. Nevertheless he immediately accepted, rising. Despite his military title—which was largely political—he never had led troops in the field; but nobody else
around there had either.

The wound was not Dickinson's from seven years earlier,
though that bullet from time to time did give him trouble.
No, this was from a more recent brawl, a four-sided affair that
had farcical aspects; and the General, who was possessed of no
sense of humor, and couldn't bear to be laughed at, may have
seized upon this excuse to get out of the state for a little while;
but most likely he would have taken the field anyway, for he
was fascinated by war and always had wanted to fight one.

There was in the militia of Tennessee at that time a tall,
handsome, quiet, but rather uppish young officer who recently
had arrived from Virginia. Jackson liked Carroll, but Carroll's
fellow subalterns didn't. One of these challenged. Carroll refused on the ground that the man, though an officer, was not a
gentleman, a distinction any Virginian was entitled to make.
Another officer challenged—it would seem that Carroll had offended the whole mess—and got the same answer. Then they

talked Jesse Benton, brother of Jackson's friend Thomas Hart Benton, a colonel, into challenging; and this challenge Carroll accepted, asking Andrew Jackson to act for him. Jackson should have refused, and he did try to do so, on the ground of age and greatly superior military rank; but Carroll couldn't get anybody else, and at last the General made the mistake of consenting.

Many ballads, all dirty, were made by this duel.

The principals were placed back to back and were told that at a signal they should step away from one another, turning, and fire at will. This sort of meeting more often than not meant death or serious injuries on both sides, since the fighters were but a few feet apart. Jesse Benton thought to avert this by crouching very low as he turned. Though of course it was customary to stand upright, there was nothing in the cartel that said he couldn't stoop. And stoop he did. He was bent almost to the ground when he fired, his opponent firing at that same instant. Benton missed. Carroll's ball skipped across Benton's bent back and tore a long strip of skin off Benton's buttocks.

For weeks afterward Benton couldn't sit down, while Tennesseans laughed until the tears came to their eyes.

Jesse wrote an account of the affair to his brother Thomas, who at that time was in Washington on General Jackson's business. Jesse intimated that Jackson had not been genteel and was the source of some of the bawdy stories that filled the frontier about his, Jesse's, backside. A prickly man at any time, Thomas Hart Benton wrote sharply to the General; and he was as sharply answered; and so these two, who until this time had been the best of friends, now became enemies. No doubt busybodies poked it, telling each man acrid tales of what his opponent said about him. This was the custom. Perhaps the General's friends even raked up some old insults to Rachel. At any rate, Andrew Jackson swore roundly that the next time he saw Thomas Hart Benton he would horsewhip him.

Soon after this Thomas Benton came to Nashville, with his brother. They put up in a hotel not ordinarily frequented by General Jackson, but the General's friends hurried right out to

The Hermitage with this snippet of gossip. The General was spending most of his time at The Hermitage these days. He wasn't feeling well, and was increasingly irritable, as he himself complained. In 1804 he had ceased to be chief justice of Tennessee, so that he was no longer on circuit, and except when his military duties took him away he could be found at The Hermitage, raising blooded horses.

Well, he got out his whip. He also pocketed a pistol, just to be sure.

With his friend, tall serious Colonel Coffee, who was married to a niece of his wife, he went downtown. As they crossed the square on the way to the post office they saw Thomas Hart Benton standing in the doorway of his inn.

"Do you see that fellow?" asked Coffee.

"Oh, yes, I have my eyes on him."

Benton would have done well to get away from there, but he didn't move, and he was still standing in the doorway when the two men returned from the post office. Jackson whirled on him, raising the horsewhip, at the same time drawing his pistol.

"Now, you damned rascal, I'm going to thrash you! Defend yourself!"

What happened after that happened very fast, and it lost nothing in the subsequent retelling.

Thomas Hart Benton stepped backward into the hotel lobby, trying to get out his own pistol, which was under his coat in front. Jackson followed, gun aimed. Out of a side door came Jesse Benton, and he too had a pistol in his hand. Believing that his brother was about to be killed, Jesse fired at Jackson, hitting the General in the left shoulder. Jackson fell. At the same time through the door behind Jackson charged Coffee, who by this time had *his* pistol out too. Coffee aimed at Thomas Hart Benton, who took still another step backward—and fell downstairs. That fall cost Benton a few bruises, but it probably saved his life. Meanwhile still another Jackson follower ran in from the street, and he knocked down Jesse (whose pistol now was empty) and began to stamp upon him with hobnailed boots, an accepted practice of the period.

So it was that Andrew Jackson, though hurt, rose gladly when they summoned him to war; for he felt that he needed a little action.

The Creeks were not a formidable foe. Scattered through scores of small villages, they could muster possibly 7,000 warriors, but only about 4,000 of these were in favor of taking to the war path; and of that 4,000—they were called Red Sticks because they carried red sticks, it is not clear why—less than one-third had muskets, while there was very little powder or lead, the Spanish governor at Pensacola, their only source of supply, doling it out skimpily, for, he said, only hunting purposes.

Yet they *were* Indians, and when in a frenzy they would maim, scalp.

Any frontiersman knew what to do.

It was not a glorious war, and not a war marked by magnanimity. Squaws and papooses generally were spared, though not always; but there were no other prisoners, on either side. Any battle was a massacre.

"Why does Jackson kill so many Indians?" somebody asked Governor Blount.

"Because he knows how," the governor replied.

There were supposed to be three white armies, one proceeding west from Georgia, one (Jackson's) south from Tennessee, and one, consisting largely of regulars, up from the Gulf coast country; but Jackson had to do the whole job himself, the mismanagement at home being even more pronounced than usual. Despite desertions and the appalling inefficiency of the supply department—"We will stay here if we have to eat acorns," Jackson said grimly at Fort Strother in the face of one more threatened mutiny—he managed to hold his army together long enough to whip the Indians at Talladega and again at Tohopeka (the Horse Shoe), causing them to plead for peace.

These victories, made largely with militia, were not brilliant; but any kind of victory looked good in Washington at that stage of the war, and Jackson's stock soared. He was offered a regular army commission of brigadier general. There were no major generalships open, but Washington promised that he would be brevetted for the next vacancy.

Jackson paused, though not for long. The truth is, he had for some time been thinking of joining the regular army. He loved the military life, and things in and around Nashville had not been going too well for him. He had made many more enemies than friends by the Benton unpleasantness, and there were even those among his neighbors who thought that he had gone a little too far when he killed Charles Dickinson in cold blood. His law practice didn't amount to much. He could hardly hope to get his justiceship back. He was dabbling in merchandise, but not doing well at it.

He even thought, at this time, of moving farther south, into the Mississippi territory, or perhaps across the river to Missouri. The frontier, after all, was shifting. Western Tennessee was getting too tame.

Just at that time William Henry Harrison, in a pet, threw up his commission, and the War Department immediately offered this, a major generalship, to Jackson. He accepted with alacrity.

He was made commanding officer of the Seventh Military District, which embraced everything then known as the Southwest, from the Mississippi to the Alleghenies, from the Ohio to the Gulf. He was sent back into the Mississippi territory to make a peace treaty with the beaten Creeks, many of whom had helped him in his campaign.

That treaty—there was no dickering, Jackson simply announced the terms, and the Indians couldn't so much as whimper—was one of the harshest in American history.

Indeed, it was so harsh that as soon as they could the Creeks would feel called upon to violate it. Jackson must have known this. But he planned to keep his army, largely regulars now, in the field. He would overawe the Spaniards in Florida, and kick out the British who had landed there, and in the process he could continue to threaten the Creeks, who would not dare to strike. As for the force that was gathering in Jamaica, it could wait.

Word was brought to the General that Colonel Nicholls in Pensacola had issued a statement that he would be in New Orleans in two months.

"There will be bloody noses before that happens," Andrew Jackson said.

Chapter 19

A PHILADELPHIA LAWYER—the occasion seemed to call for one —had been installed in the Treasury. After Albert Gallatin had gone off to Europe the Senate refused to confirm his appointment as a peace commissioner on the ground that he couldn't be that and Secretary of the Treasury at the same time; so he was induced from afar to resign his Secretaryship, and the President appointed in his place an old-time office-holder who happened at that moment to be out of office, George W. Campbell of Tennessee. Campbell doubtless did the best he could, but when Congress met in special session September 19, 1814, using the Post and Patent Office building, the only unburned public structure in Washington, he had to report that there was less than $5 million in the till. By means of a series of extraordinary and quite possibly impractical methods, he added, he *thought* that this *might* be raised to $24 million. But—$74 million was immediately needed. Where the balance of $50 million was coming from, Campbell said, he couldn't imagine. Then he resigned; and they called in the attorney from Philadelphia.

This was Alexander James Dallas, a man caustic, laconic,

and not well liked, but a man of courage withal. Spewing sarcasm, Dallas pitched in.

He had little enough to work with, and certainly no confidence on the part of the public. There wasn't a federal banking system any more, and state and private banks were closing right and left after the burning of Washington, while those that remained open, always excepting the New England ones, resolutely suspended specie payments.

This, together with the approach of the Hartford convention, made it look more than likely that the country might collapse at any moment. The dictator of the Southwest, Andrew Jackson, did not know whether he would be able to pay his troops. Communications being what they were, he didn't know, at any given time, whether he still had a government behind him. But he proceeded as though he did have. He went to Mobile.

There was another Cabinet change after Bladensburg. Though General Winder was not Armstrong's choice in the first place, and had been forced upon him by the President, and though Armstrong was almost the only high government official in that terrible campaign who had kept his head, there must be a scapegoat. Armstrong wasn't a fool. He was not *asked* to resign, at least he wasn't asked publicly; but he knew who was running the government, and he knew too that for a long while the impatient James Monroe had wanted the War Department; so he did resign, and he went home. Monroe got the job first as an *ad interim* appointee, but after a month this was made permanent. Monroe did not cease to be Secretary of State. Fearful that New York would be angry—and Federalist sentiment seemed to be growing in New York, which might conceivably join New England in the big walkout—President Madison hastened to offer the State Department to Governor Tompkins. But the canny governor said no. A Cabinet run by Virginians, he decided, was no place for a New York man.

When Jackson reached Mobile, August 15, he was still reporting to John Armstrong. He then had under his command five regiments of regulars, all infantry, the 2nd, 3rd, 7th, 39th, and 44th, besides some 350 artillerists—a little over 2,000 men in all.[29] When he heard of what was happening in Pensacola he thought he needed more, so he wrote to his friend Governor Blount of Tennessee, asking for 2,500 militia. He wrote too to Don Matteo Gonzales Manrique, the Spanish governor at Pensacola, warning him that there must be no more assistance to the fugitive Creeks, "a murderous barbarous rebellious Banditti [30] who have not only imbued their hands in the innocent blood of our defenseless women and children, but raised the exterminating Hatchet against their own nation." He wrote to the Secretary of War, reporting this letter. The date was August 30, the very day that John Armstrong ceased to hold that job and James Monroe took over. That same day, in Mobile, General Jackson got a long and elaborately abusive answer from Don Matteo.

September 27—this was how the General learned that he had a new boss—Secretary Monroe wrote to General Jackson warning him that the British were massing in great numbers in the West Indies, undoubtedly for a descent upon Louisiana. A week before, the General had received a memorial from the newly formed citizens' defense committee of New Orleans, of which his old friend in Congress, Edward Livingston, was an active member. There was also a personal letter from Livingston. These both begged him to go to New Orleans and personally to see to the defenses of that city.

Jackson wasn't interested. Mobile was near the twitchy Creeks: New Orleans would be much too far away. The Red Sticks in his mind at that moment were more important than the redcoats. Granted that the British planned to strike for New Orleans, wasn't it perfectly obvious that they would disembark at Mobile, if they could, and march overland to some river point above the Crescent City—say Baton Rouge or even Natchez—thus avoiding all that triply treacherous delta country? It was obvious to Andrew Jackson anyway. He had said it first thing, and he kept saying it. He was not a man who readily changed his mind.

October 21, having meanwhile received Jackson's letter telling about the correspondence with Don Matteo, Secretary Monroe wrote again. He was suave, tactful, for the General's temper was known and feared as far away as Washington. "The President approves the manly tone with which you have asserted the rights of your country in your correspendence with the Governor of that province," but "A minister having lately been appointed on our part, to that Government,[31] and our relations with it being amicable, it is deemed more proper, that a representation of the insolent and unjustifiable conduct of the Governor of Pensacola, should be made to that Government thro' the Ordinary channels of communication then that you should resent it by an attack on Pensacola." [32]

In other words, give us a chance to try diplomacy first.

Andrew Jackson had little use for diplomacy. Long before he got that letter he had pounced upon Pensacola.

Though strictly illegal, the feat was not a difficult one. Jackson had the men, having been heavily reinforced from Tennessee and by local levees; there were some 3,000 of them, even after the cavalry, for lack of grass in Florida, had to be left behind on the banks of the Alabama; and the march was easy. The garrison, as Jackson's spies already had informed him, was but a token one. The British were several miles out of town, at a place called the Barrancas, and they too were represented only by a token force, seven small vessels.

Madison's craving for Florida, like Monroe's, was so well known that Spain, which could not send an army across the sea, and which was having trouble holding onto what was left of its American empire, would do everything possible to refrain from giving the United States any excuse for war.

Furthermore, Jackson had a threat. His Choctaw scouts, trifling in number, and easily handled, must be put to their fullest use.

"I will not hold myself responsible for the conduct of my enraged soldiers and warriors," he wrote in a message that called upon the governor to surrender the city.

Thus he did the same thing, almost to the word, that Brock had done to Hull at Detroit. The British, truly, had worked this trick many more times than had the Americans; but the British had more Indians.

The message never got there. Don Matteo no doubt figured that he should make at least a show of resistance, Spanish honor being what it was; and the bearer of the white flag was fired upon—and retreated.

It was too late in the afternoon to do anything more that day, November 6, but first thing in the morning Jackson sent about 500 men around to the west of the city in a feint, and before the British could guess what he was up to and bring their naval guns to bear upon him he was driving into Pensacola from the east. The fight was short and not notably sharp: the Spaniards, overwhelmingly outnumbered, surrendered almost immediately.

What they surrendered, it was stipulated, *what* the American force would have command of until such a time as Spain could send sufficient reinforcements to enable the garrison to live up to the Spanish obligation of neutrality, included all arms—and of course it included the fort, Barrancas.

But the British had Barrancas, and the British had other ideas. Before Jackson could go after them the next day they blew up the fort and sailed away. Jackson was furious, berating the governor. Jackson never was a good loser.

In truth it left him in rather a ridiculous position. Without authority he had invaded a foreign possession, but his real enemy, his excuse, had escaped; and his real object, the fort, was in ruins. He had chased away Nicholls, yes; but Nicholls, whom Jackson had been treating as an eagle, never was meant to be more than an annoying gnat. Jackson had perhaps impressed with his strength the Indian allies of the British, the Seminoles and fugitive Creeks, but he had very little use for Indians anyway. To rebuild and to garrison Fort Barrancas was beyond his means, if he meant to hold it.

As a matter of fact, there wasn't anything left for him to do but go back to Mobile; and this he did.

The fleet between the Negril points at the western end of Jamaica was too big for that bay to hold. It was swollen, and it strained. General Brooke and Admiral Malcolm (yet another Scottish admiral!) had brought the bulk of the Chesapeake Bay force on November 1. On November 19 there had arrived from Halifax Admiral Cochrane and another fleet, another huge force of soldiers. November 21, a little late, came five companies of the Rifle Brigade (3rd battalion) from France, by way of Plymouth, and the 93rd Highlanders, Sutherlanders, a crack outfit, from the Cape of Good Hope, also by way of Plymouth. And there were smaller groups, there and on the way: the 1st West India regiment, the 5th West India regiment, 200 Negro pioneers, besides marines and available fighting seamen to the number of about 1,500.

It was a glorious sight, there in the tropical sun. There were more than fifty vessels, ranging from the enormous high-sided *Carron* to that saucy small sloop *Pigmy*. They had a review, bands playing, all flags flying, November 25; and the next day they sailed.

Four days before that, November 22, Andrew Jackson had left Mobile. He was going to New Orleans at last.

Chapter 20

LANGUOROUS WAS the word for New Orleans. Sprawled in the mud between river and swamp, a wet hot site, she was dusky, and her voice was husky, and there was something foreign and faintly disreputable about her—something that fascinated. Yes, languorous. And a little lopsided.

The city never before had been exposed to democracy, and its inhabitants were not sure that they approved the process. They were a suspicious, supercilious, withdrawn lot, leery of the rest of the world and even of one another. Predominately

French in origin—the Spanish influence, excepting in architecture, was slight—yet they did not come from any *one part* of France; and their long colonial experience, so far from simplifying social distinctions, as it had done along the Atlantic coast, considerably complicated these.

There were many Dominicans in New Orleans in 1814, fugitives from their own island, where there had been a terrible slave uprising, reluctant to go back to the mother country while the political scene was so uncertain, or else inured to the indolent life of the semitropics. They were called *colons,* and they even had their own loafing place in New Orleans, the Café des Réfugiés, between Dumaine and St. Philip streets, near the market. Many of these people were rich and had their own slaves.

Yet there were a great many manumitted Negroes in New Orleans, the so-called free-men-of-color, and this alarmed old inhabitants, for the city was touchy about the chance of an uprising, in part perhaps because of the very presence of those *colons,* some of whom had gruesome tales to tell; so that when at the approach of war—or rather at the *realization* of the approach of war, which in fact had been in existence for some time, though few New Orleanaise had given it thought—it was suggested that a company or even a regiment be formed out of those Negroes (with white officers, of course), the cry of protest was shrill. There were plantation districts not far from the city where the population was as high as fifty-to-one black. No owner of such a plantation could look save in horror at a proposal to put guns into Negro hands; and there were many living in the city itself who felt the same way. They had been brought up to expect Negroes to do practically everything for them—everything but fight. The project, then, might have frittered away, had it not been for the sharp intervention of Andrew Jackson, who from a distance—Mobile—wrote to the city he had not yet deigned to visit, a command that such Negro outfits be raised. And that was that, a rebuff to the Crescent City. The General even issued a special and especially polysyllabic proclamation to the free-men-of-color.

New Orleans must have been the *duelingest* city in the world. On a given morning, regardless of the weather, which was usually bad, in St. Anthony's Square just behind the Cathedral, at Les Trois Capelines on the Metarie Road, or, later, under the live oaks on Louis Allard's plantation barely outside of town, you might see as many as half a dozen punctiliously arranged murder attempts in progress. New Orleanaise fought over anything or over nothing at all, purely for the fun of it. In certain circles, the more enviable ones, it was thought that there was something odd about a man who never had been on the field of honor. He was looked at askance.

And yet again, things were different in New Orleans. At a time when in other Southern or Latin cities the pistol was coming to be accepted as *the* dueling weapon—it was the only one used elsewhere in the United States, or even thought of— the fire-eaters of New Orleans clung to the romantic sword. Not infrequently they carried sword canes, for it was a rough city and not safe after dark. They used foils in the academies, and in the field épées, or, sometimes, the *colchemard,* a pointed and edged blade something like a short rapier.

The fencing master was a New Orleans hero, a figure of chivalry, the subject of many a tale. They were pointed out, and mentioned with awe or with affection, those glittering personages—Bonneval, l'Alouette, Pepe Lulla, Beaudoin, "Titi" Rosiere, Emile Cazere. The most talked-about and most powerful of them all, who was also known as the handsomest man in town and a great dandy, was a mulatto (the French West Indies blood classification of *mulâtre, quarteron, métis* or *octavon, mamelouque, sang-mélé, griffe, sacatra,* and *marabou* was maintained in New Orleans, no doubt because of the Santo Domingan influence). This was the redoubtable Bastile Croquere, whose fencing academy at Exchange Alley and Conti Street was not only something of a museum—the man's collection of cameos was stunning—but was also the meeting place of many of the young aristocrats in town, his pupils. Croquere probably trained more youths for duels than any other master in Louisiana, though he could not himself take part in one of

these, either as principal or second, since he was not, technically,
a gentleman.

As to massed, organized, uniformed slaughter, however, New
Orleans was not so zealous. It had not until now been threatened. The Indians in those parts, Houmas and Natchez, were
a pusillanimous pack. There never had been in New Orleans
the horrid feeling of threat that other frontier towns and
cities knew. Personal courage, yes. Gallantry, of course. But
apprehensiveness, discipline—that was something different. The
militia, under General Villeré, a planter south of the city, was
far under its quota, and poor even as it stood. There were
certain gay outfits, exclusive groups for officers, with bright
costumes—the Feliciana Dragoons, Plauché's Guards—and they
could do a pert drill in the Place d'Armes, the very center
of the city, its heart, thrilling Sunday onlookers; but to any
soldier they must have looked like toys on a nursery floor.

More important, the Orleanaise did not like this war. It
was costing them money, to no purpose. They couldn't see
any sense in it. They were disinclined to rally 'round a group
of coarse Northerners to whom they had recently and forcibly
been attached. And they were increasingly hurt by the non-
appearance of the commander in chief of this district. New
Orleans, sir, should be treated with more respect.

"The Legislature have not as yet done anything to damp
the public ardour," Governor Claiborne reported to Jackson,
November 16, almost with relief. "I hope this body will be
justly impressed with the dangers to which we are exposed,
and will warmly second all my efforts; But I fear, I much fear,
they will not act with the promptitude and the Energy which
the crisis demands." [33]

The residents of New Orleans were split into many sects,
many classes and cliques, and they quarrelled among themselves; but there was one thing upon which they were united,
and that was hatred of the Kaintucks.

There were two kinds of visitors, neither very desirable.
Those who came from the South, up the river, were sailors,
members of many nations, and no worse, if no better, than

sailors elsewhere in the world were expected to be. But those who came from the North, down the river—customarily in keelboats or flatboats or broadhorns, but some on rafts—were the Kaintucks (though by no means all or even most of them actually did come from Kentucky). A Kaintuck was the lowest of the low. New Orleanaise were not narrow-minded; and they could make allowance for rough backwoodsmen who after weeks and even months of terrible labor with poles at last reached New Orleans with all its brash pleasures, and were paid off and sent ashore so that the keelboat or whatnot could be sold for firewood. But the Kaintucks, by and large, were even worse than that. They were vermin, and extremely malodorous vermin to boot.

New Orleans was beginning to burst out of its early limits, the founded square, the Vieux Carre, which was formed by the river, the Esplanade, the ruined old wall on Rampart Street, and the Faubourg Ste. Marie. That last, located right in the old city moat—it was sometimes called simply The Swamp [34]—was a shantytown of bars, bordellos, and boarding-houses that catered to boatmen. The trouble was, the boatmen didn't always stay there. Out of The Swamp, from time to time, would come a miasmatic upsurging of Kaintucks on a rampage, to make decent folks afraid to go forth. The Kain-tucks could be dangerous when drunk, and they usually were drunk; but even sober they were despicable. Never trust a Kaintuck, men would tell you in New Orleans. Never get near one if you could help it.

And now the city, unashamedly excited, was waiting for the arrival of the man who so far had snubbed it—Andrew Jackson.

And Jackson was a Kaintuck.

Chapter 21

HE TOOK HIS time. He sent a strong detachment, mostly horse-men, under Major Blue, to operate against the remaining Creeks along the Escambia, and to destroy Nicholls' supply posts on the Apalachicola. He assigned the Georgia militia, on its way west, to Mobile, which he still esteemed the key to the whole military situation; and there too, in Mobile, he left the 2nd, 3rd, and 39th regiments, about 1,100 men; but he commanded the 44th to follow him.

The ordinary means of going from Mobile to New Orleans was by inland waterway; but the General went horseback, with only a small body of aides, in order, as he wrote to Secretary Monroe, "to have a view of the points at which the enemy might effect a landing." It was proof of his conscientiousness, if further proof could be called for, since he was seriously ill at the time with dysentery.

He made it in easy stages, leaving Mobile November 22, getting to New Orleans (about 120 miles, the way he rode) December 1.

Many other groups were converging upon the Crescent City at that moment. Across the placid Gulf of Mexico from the southeast came the British armada, with all its bells and bugles, its gun drills and gambling, a mighty, ponderous, slow-paced array. The General's friend, Coffee, a brigadier now, had joined him in Mobile on October 25 with somewhat more than the 2,500 Tennessee militiamen Jackson had called for, and Coffee's column, or most of it, was to proceed to Baton Rouge, from which it might be summoned to New Orleans at any hour. Yet another Tennessee force, the second division of the militia, some 2,000 strong, or a little more, under Major General Carroll, was on its way south, as was too a force of more than 2,000 Kentuckians under General Thomas. The Secretary of War, as he told Jackson in a letter, had scraped up $100,000 in gold and sent this to Governor Blount of Tennessee to be forwarded to the chief of the 7th military district; and this Blount had done, by special messenger, who was even now on his way. At the same time the Secretary of War had arranged to have placed aboard a boat at Pittsburgh for shipment down the Ohio and Mississippi rivers to New Orleans a large supply of muskets and ammunition, besides several thousand blankets. Jackson desperately needed these, for the nights were nippy; but in order to save money they had been shipped not by an expensive steamboat but by a keelboat, the skipper of which stopped at every hamlet along the banks in order to do a little trade.

It was a cold wet morning, with a mizzling rain, when Andrew Jackson rode into New Orleans.

He came from the north, having breakfasted with a certain Mr. Kilty, a trader, whose house was out near where the Carondelet Canal and Bayou St. Jean came together.

New Orleans looked at him, and was not amused.

A carriage had been sent out to the city limits to meet him, but he spurned this, staying on his horse. There no doubt he was well advised, for he was an admirable horseman. But as far as New Orleans was concerned, that first wet morning, his merits went no further.

New Orleans loved a show, a parade, and the city fathers had done the best they could on short notice. Plauché's Guards were there, and St. Gême's carabiniers, and the chasseurs of Captain Guibert, while immediately around the General himself, forming his bodyguard, his guard of honor, were the glittering, shimmering, blue-and-silver Feliciana Dragoons. In the middle of all this the commanding officer of the Seventh United States Military District cut a drab figure.

A conquering hero should smirk—or glare. He should clank with medals, gleam with gold lace. This one, from the neck up, save for his direct, damn-you eyes, could have been a *memento mori,* a death's-head. He was angular, all joints. His back was a ramrod. A worn leather cap was on his head, a short Spanish cloak of faded blue cloth was across his shoulders and had been frogged over his chest against the chill, hiding his insignia and decorations, if he had any. He was tired, damn it. His boots, which had not been polished in a week, flapped senselessly against scarecrow knees.

In short, he fitted the day, though not the company.

He turned his head neither to right nor to left, nor did he raise and lower it in acknowledgment of the scattered, half-scared, half-derisive cheers by which he was greeted.

Thus he rode, staring straight ahead, with no prance, no clack. And then he was gone.

Scarcely able to sit in saddle, but unwilling to let this show, he went to previously prepared quarters in Royal Street, where he plunged into business.

The city may have been disappointed in his appearance, at least that first morning, but it was at no time unaware of his presence. It had needed him, craved him. A driver, who thought nothing of working fourteen hours a day, and couldn't see why everybody else didn't, he was in a position to stiffen and to co-ordinate the rather wan, rather flabby preparations for defense. He knew what he wanted, and he meant to get it.

He met the governor, William C. C. Claiborne, a tall, thin, very serious young Virginian, with whom he had been corresponding from the field. They did not like one another personally, these two, but they worked well together.

He met his old friend Edward Livingston, and was invited to a reception at Livingston's home that night.

At the reception, he met somewhat more than a sprinkling of blue-blooded belles, and to their amazement, though not to his own, he charmed them. This Yanqui might be bluff with his fellow men; he had a tongue of tabasco when anything went wrong at headquarters or on the parade ground; but in the presence of ladies he was invariably, instinctively courtly. That night, shaved, powdered, his boots shined at last, and wearing his dress uniform, he made a good impression, bowing, saying the proper things. The belles agreed, afterward, that no matter what folks said about Andrew Jackson he was a real gentleman when once you got to know him.

This helped, in New Orleans.

He met the ranking naval officer of the district, a man who had recently uprooted the pirate camp on Grande Terre, Master-Commander Daniel Todd Patterson, a short, stocky, bluff, no-fooling fellow, who in a few words described the situation from where he stood.[35]

There was a sloop-of-war, *Louisiana,* in harbor. Her master was Lieutenant C. B. Thompson, and she carried sixteen long 24-pounders, a heavy armament for those waters. There was also at New Orleans a schooner-of-war, *Carolina,* 14 guns, of which Patterson himself was master. Out at Tchifonte, on Lake Pontchartrain, there was in process of construction a large flat-bottomed frigate—the lake was shallow—designed to carry forty-two guns. This vessel when finished would patrol New Orleans' aquatic back yard; but it was not yet finished; the guns hadn't been mounted, a mighty job. As she stood, then, for the present, this frigate was no asset but rather a liability, since, while she was building and being readied, a shallow-draft brig, *Aetna,* had to be told off to guard her, lest the invading British seize her; and that brig could have been used elsewhere.

In addition there were six of Mr. Jefferson's absurd gunboats—they didn't even have names, only numbers—and two one-gun sloops, *Seahorse* and *Alligator.* These would be no good for any manner of combat, and were meant only to act as scouts. One of the gunboats was stationed at Fort St. Philip, about fifty miles downriver from New Orleans, while the other five were off the Gulf opening of Lake Borgne, under the command of Lieutenant Thomas ap Catesby Jones.

"The Gun Boats on the Lakes will prevent the British from approaching in that quarter," General Jackson confidently wrote to Monroe, showing how little he knew of naval matters.

He met the engineers with whom he would have to work,

and he listened attentively to what they said. The General did not pretend to know anything about military engineering— how could he?—but he had the profoundest admiration for those who did. At all times they were personages of importance at headquarters. As some men are fascinated by opera stars, some by surgeons, or authors, so it was with Andrew Jackson and the engineers. He trusted them. And at New Orleans he had every reason to. His staff in that respect was excellent.

The day after his arrival he reviewed the local militia, a sorry lot, in the Place d'Armes. He congratulated them on their appearance. Cleaned up, he made a better showing; nor was it as dismal a day as yesterday had been. The General even made a speech, which Livingston interpreted, since few of the residents of New Orleans could understand English, and General Jackson didn't have a word of French.

He was not a man for pomp and public display, no balcony ranter; and thereafter they saw him seldom in New Orleans, amid the looped grillwork of which his was from time to time an incongruous figure, as he hurried from place to place. But they heard about him. A stream of emphatic orders issued from the office in Royal Street.

For example, when the assistant paymaster of that particular military district, a wretch named Allen, had the temerity to balk at the prospect of passing out cash to non-Caucasians, he was brought up short by the General himself:

Be pleased to keep to yourself your Opinions upon the policy of making payments to particular Corps. It is enough for you to receive my order for the payment of the troops with the necessary muster rolls without inquiring whether the troops are white, Black, or Tea. You are not to know whether I have received authority from the War Department to employ any particular description of men, and will, upon the receipt of this make payments of the Choctaws upon the musters rolls of Major Blue.[36]

Yes, he was inflexible in the matter of nonwhite recruits, but he changed his mind about the Baratarians. In Mobile he had called them "hellish Banditti," but it was different now that he realized how badly he needed gunners. Also, there was his friend Livingston, attached to his staff as an unpaid volunteer with the rank of lieutenant colonel. Livingston was working for the Lafittes, and Livingston, more than any other man, had the ear of the General.

Jean and Pierre Lafitte were only half in hiding. They did not dare to swagger in public, as before; but everybody knew that they were nearby. Technically outlaws, they yet did not hesitate to file suit against the federal government for recovery of the property seized at Grande Terre, hiring for this purpose not only Livingston but also John R. Grymes, who resigned his post as district attorney of Orleans Parish to take the case—at a reported fee of $20,000.

Never mind their past, the Baratarians were to be recruited. It is not likely that Jean Lafitte confronted General Jackson in person, though the romantic residents of New Orleans preferred to think that it had happened that way. But somehow the agreement was reached that pirates, just now, could join in the defense.

The General dropped down the river, his first real look at the delta country, to Fort St. Philip. He ordered some more guns mounted there, and then he went back to New Orleans, examining both banks carefully as he did so.

He still did not believe that the thrust would be directly at New Orleans. He clung to his belief that the British would first seize Mobile, then march overland to a point perhaps near Baton Rouge or Natchez or even as far north as the Walnut Hills.[37] That this would mean cutting themselves off from their base, and venturing deep, without heavy guns, into enemy country, not rich country either, that it would mean foregoing the tremendous assistance the Navy could give in the amphibious techniques the British had built up over the years and that were peculiarly their own—this made no difference to Andrew Jackson, who had made up his mind.

Even when he heard that a vast British flotilla had appeared off Cat Island and Ship Island at the entrance of Lake Borgne —it was not a lake, really, but a lagoon, a landlocked arm of the sea—he still wasn't flustered.

"I expect this is a Faint," he wrote to Coffee.

He was never more mistaken in his life.

Chapter 22

BACK IN THE CITY, he told Governor Claiborne and Mayor Girod once again what he thought of their militia—and it was not like the formal praise that Livingston had interpreted. The quota allotted to Louisiana under the call of 1814 for 90,000 volunteers was 1,960. Nowhere in the country had the quota been filled, but nowhere had enlistments been so woefully weak as in Louisiana. Fewer than 600 volunteers paraded before Andrew Jackson the day after his arrival, and more than a third of those were Santo Domingans. It looked as though these folks just didn't *want* to be saved.

He left the city again, this time to inspect the defense works to the north and east.

If the British meant business, down there by Cat and Ship Islands, if they really were about to invade, this would be the way they'd come.

Most of the area was swamp or open water. There were only two possible avenues of approach to the city.

East of New Orleans, beyond the suburb of Marigny—that is, downriver, for the Mississippi flows virtually west-to-east at this point—was a succession of small plantations, mostly in sugar and cotton, lying between the levee and the thick cypress swamp. It was a flat, well-cultivated, easily traveled strip, about a mile wide. But it would be difficult of access from the north or the east. It was, to all intents and purposes, an island, that plantation strip. The enemy could hardly get to it.

True, the swamp was stripped with bayous that flowed—if "flowed" is the word—from the Mississippi to Lake Borgne; but these, always low and narrow, now were the lowest that any man could remember having seen them, so that it was believed that no considerable military body, complete with cannons, could use any one of them. Nevertheless Jackson ordered that each one be blocked by fallen trees.

Then he went to the Chef Menteur road. This was really a road, and a singularly solid one for that part of the world, running from the north of the city northeast along a thin but amazingly high (again, for that part of the world) strip of land known as the Plain of Gentilly. It went to Lake Borgne, which in turn was directly connected with the sound between the Chandeleur Islands, the British fleet's landfall, and Mobile.

It was the Chef Menteur road, his engineers told the General —and he quickly came to agree—that the British would take, if they came at all. There were already several batteries there. Jackson ordered more.

He was engaged in this work when the news came that the five gunboats under Lieutenant ap Catesby Jones, which upon the approach of the British had retreated into the shallow waters of Lake Borgne, had been attacked from barges—and taken. The Americans, enormously outnumbered, had fought well; but every one of them was either dead or a prisoner.

So *that* gate stood wide open.

The General hurried back to New Orleans. He sent to Coffee at Baton Rouge an order to come to New Orleans immediately with all his men. He sent similar orders, hurry-up orders of an emergency nature, to Carroll and the second Tennessee militia division and to Thomas and his Kentuckians, wherever they were—nobody seemed to know—upriver somewhere. He issued a proclamation telling the people of Louisiana to behave themselves, and warning them that he would not hesitate to take full authority, suspending all other, if in his opinion they didn't. He sent to the legislature a request that that body immediately suspend the writ of habeas corpus, and when the legislature hesitated he proclaimed martial law.

The British weren't the only ones who meant business.

The British, as a matter of fact, had been having almost unbelievably bad luck. They were delayed at the rendezvous, awaiting the arrival of their new commander-in-chief, and they had finally sailed, several days late, without him. At first the command had been slated for General Ross, and when Ross was killed before Baltimore the plan itself was not changed in any way but it was necessary to send out a new commanding officer. This was being done, the men at Negril Bay learned. The chief even then was on his way across the Atlantic, complete with staff, aboard the *Statira*. The rumor was that this was the Iron Duke himself. Meanwhile, the expedition was under the command of Major General John Keane. Now, Keane was a good man, and he had his orders, but it was not inspiriting to reflect that any day, indeed at almost any hour, he was to be superseded by some highly connected favorite who would get all the glory.

They had left Negril Bay November 22, and did not arrive off the Chandeleurs until December 10. This additional delay was caused by a series of headwinds, climaxed, almost within sight of land, by a blow that could be called a hurricane—it scattered them. With typical British doggedness they got together again. They were old-timers, these invading men, and tough.

Then they met the gunboats. These would not fight any of the vessels the British had. They weren't meant to. Yet neither might they be ignored. From the place to which they had retreated they could make impossible a large movement of troops across Lake Borgne in small boats—and the movement would *have* to be made in small boats. So the gunboats must be knocked out. This was done, but only at an expectedly great expense of labor and men—and time.

The gunboat battle was December 14, though news of it did not reach General Jackson until the next day.

The British promptly landed an advance force under Colonel Thornton. These were crack troops, from various outfits. Most of them had met Americans in the field, and had no use for them as fighters: Thornton himself was the man who led the charge at Bladensburg, that walkover. Despite rain and a raw cutting wind, their spirits were high when, after a backbreaking pull across Lake Borgne, at last they scrambled and slushed ashore at Isle aux Pois.

Even in good weather it would have been a bleak prospect. There was no shelter, no cover, no fuel with which to build fires—and the rain never paused.

Teeth chattering, stomachs wambling, their eyes red from sleeplessness, they remained in that place for four days and four nights.[38] And then they had their first break, which must have loomed as a miracle.

Dismayed by news of the unprecedentedly low water in the bayous, they had sent out an advance guard of their own, a couple of young and energetic officers, one Navy, Captain P. Spencer, one Army, Lieutenant John Peddie, of the 27th Infantry (who, incidentally, was deputy assistant quartermaster general of the whole expedition). These two, on December 18, went in a small boat from Isle aux Pois to the very head of the Lake, where, at the mouth of Bayou Bienvenu, they found a fishing village.

The fishermen were Spanish, and they had no love for Yanquis. They told the officers that Bayou Bienvenu, unlike all the others, and unaccountably, had not been blocked by fallen trees. Even then, it would take an expert guide to reach the plantations along the edge of the Mississippi. Would they do it? Would they, for some coins, take the officers there? *Si, si, señores.*[39]

A little later—they could hardly believe their eyes—the terrain had about it a fairy-tale haziness—the two officers stood on the edge of the Villeré plantation, on the river itself not more than nine miles from New Orleans.

There was not an American soldier in sight, and there was no sort of fortification.

The British officers, peering out of the brush, weren't seen. They returned to the fishing village and then to Isle aux Pois, taking all the fishermen with them.

This advance guard was known for the occasion as the 22nd light brigade, and it consisted of 1,688 rank and file, almost all of them veterans, navy, army, and a few marines. It started out that very night, for all of its miseries, at midnight, and approached the village at the mouth of the Bayou Bienvenu at dawn. The village, unexpectedly, was occupied. A picket of U.S. Army regulars, a sergeant and eight privates, had moved in the previous afternoon. Why they were so late, as why the trees had not been felled across this particular bayou, nobody seemed to know—or to care. The soldiers saw nothing unusual about the deserted village: no doubt the fishermen were all out fishing. They simply made themselves at home; and they were asleep when the 22nd light brigade took over.

It was about noon, a muggy, typically close midday in the delta country, when the 22nd light brigade stole out of the swamp and into the Villeré plantation. Nothing stirred, not so much as a butterfly. On the veranda of the plantation house, head back, a handkerchief over his face, feet on the railing, sat —and snoozed—a lithe young man. Nobody could have been less prepared for attack. They had to wake him in order to tell him that he was a prisoner.

This was Gabriel Villeré, a major in the Louisiana militia— and his father, who owned this plantation, was a general, the commanding officer of the militia.

It was very embarrassing.

Wide awake at last, to find his ancestral acres inundated by redcoats, with more appearing all the time, young Villeré thought fast. He knew that there wasn't as much as a picket between this veranda and the Place d'Armes. He knew that General Jackson had not the faintest thought that the British were at his doorstep. Jackson must be told! Villeré wrenched himself free, vaulted the railing, and with his head low raced for the swamp.

They fired after him; but he made it.

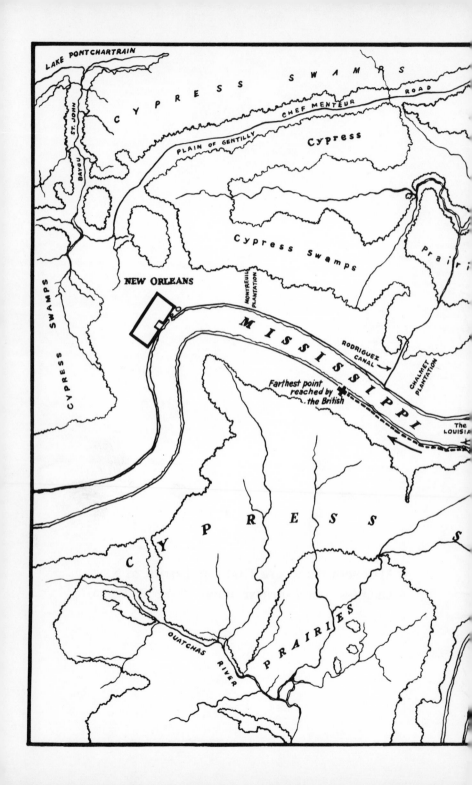

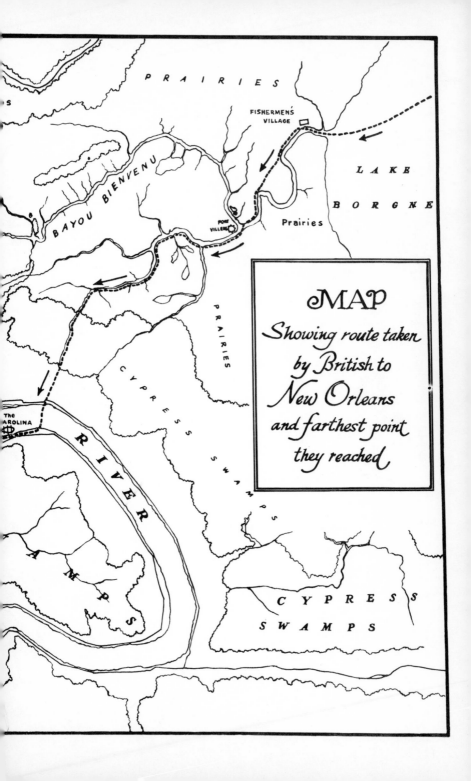

PRAIRIES

FISHERMEN'S
VILLAGE

BAYOU BIENVENU

FORT
VILLERÉ

Prairies

PRAIRIES

LAKE

BORGNE

CYPRESS SWAMPS

RIVER

The
CAROLINA

S WAMPS

CYPRESS

SWAMPS

MAP

Showing route taken
by British to
New Orleans
and farthest point
they reached

The British went no farther. They distrusted that swamp, which the young escapee doubtless knew well. They were tired, wet, hungry: they hadn't had hot food in almost a week, and there was plenty of firewood here. More men were coming up all the time, and more would continue to come, for the main body had been notified and even now General Keane was on his way in person.

The responsibility was Thornton's, and nobody ever had accused Thornton of timidity. The British could have marched those few last flat dry miles and taken New Orleans in time for tea, as easily as they had taken the Villeré plantation here. But— how could they know it?

The thing looked too good to be true. It smelled of a trap. Whatever kind of general this man Jackson was, he couldn't —he simply *could not*—be so stupid as to leave a clear un-blocked path right up to his headquarters. Maybe he was waiting for them. Those captured privates and the sergeant, back at the fishing village, had been questioned thoroughly, and separately; yet they were agreed that Jackson had at least 20,000 men in and immediately around New Orleans. (He had about a tenth of this number: the members of the picket were making up for their unalertness.) This was what the servants at the plantation house said, too.

Maybe it might be better to let General Keane make the decision.

The British posted pickets, and they began to build camp-fires.

It was about three o'clock in the afternoon when Major Villeré and his friend Dussau de la Croix, both breathless, were admitted into the presence of the commanding officer of the 7th military district, at 106 Royal Street.

Villeré had brought along de la Croix because he knew some English, whereas Villeré himself had none. De la Croix, how-ever, in his excitement, had a hard time interpreting, and it was some while before Andrew Jackson could understand what was being reported.

When he did, his face went pale, as well it might, for did ever a general find himself in such a position? [40]

He could have excused himself and gone into the next room and shot himself through the brain. But he didn't. Instead he called for his sword, and he called for his horse.

"By God, gentlemen," he cried, "we'll fight them tonight! Right now!"

Chapter 23

IT MIGHT HAVE been madness, in a few hours to scrape together a force that consisted largely of raw levees, and to hurl this, in a failing light, on an open plain, against the cream of the finest army in the world. Thornton had the 85th, the 95th, 100 sappers, a company of rocketeers, and for reserve the 4th regiment of foot.[41] Jackson had an untried rabble of about the same size. But Jackson also had imagination. In war the unexpected often is the best thing. And this, though magnificent, *was* war.

Only a company of 60 marines, some city militiamen, and two regiments of regulars, the 44th, 331 muskets, and the 7th, 465 muskets, were barracked inside of the city. But others got there, at the double. Coffee had left his sick and all of his baggage, many of his rank and file as well, at Baton Rouge, and with 800 picked men he was now at the Avart plantation about four miles north of the city, where Carroll and his Tennesseans also were encamped. Jackson ordered Carroll's outfit to the Chef Menteur road, for he thought that this Villeré plantation force was a feint; but Coffee's men came quickly into town. Plauché's battalion was brought in from Bayou St. John, about two miles from headquarters. Patterson dropped down the river in *Carolina*, her guns run out and ready. Most of the militia were out on the Chef Menteur road, the Plain of Gentilly, and Jackson kept them there; but he did call in the free men of color, the Santo Domingans. Twenty-two artillerists manned the two 6-pounders—which was more, at that, than the British presently had. There was a company of Mississippi horse under the dashing Major Hinds. And at the head of the column, as it assembled on Montreuil's plantation just below the city, were the eager youngsters of Beale's Rifles, expert shots, all local, all volunteers: they wore blue hunting shirts and wide-brimmed black felt hats.

The sun was low and the shadows long when this band set forth. A mist was creeping in from the river.

The first thing they saw of the British were their campfires gleaming in the dusk.

On their left, as they marched, the moss-hung swamp was a mass of shadow. On their right were the river and the two levees, the farther one the new one. The river was very low, and the batture—the space between the new levee and the water itself—was exceptionally wide, perhaps 150 feet: some of the campfires were on the batture, though it must have been miry there.

The field itself was bare, mostly cut cane, a harsh stubble. There were no trees. Except for an occasional irrigation ditch there was nothing behind which or in which to take cover.

So they went to battle, exuberantly. There were no feeling-outs, no flourishes; there was no hesitation either.

The British were astonished, but they were not surprised. They had never expected anything like this, yet they were prepared for it all the same, being good soldiers. The heroes of Vittoria, Badajoz, Salamanca, were not likely to be caught off-guard.

It was a weird battle and one in which many rules were broken. The *Carolina* started it, blasting away from the river, so that hundreds of the redcoats had to hug the land side of the levees. The British outposts behaved properly, firing and falling back, but neither they nor the forces sent forward to stiffen them supposed, just at first, that this was anything but a conventional, small harassment, the sort of thing that they could handle without effort. Who ever heard of a full-scale attack in these circumstances? Even the Dirty Shirts—it was their name for American militiamen—would not be *that* crack-brained.

Yet Jackson's men came right in, pell-mell. They didn't seem to know that they were doing it the wrong way.

The British fell back. But first they made a rush that caused the Americans to drag their 6-pounders to the rear, fearing that these might be taken.

The sun was gone now, and there was no moon, as there were no stars. The mist had thickened, and it was low, writhing in languid, baffled coils. The flashes of musket fire lit a terrible scene, a fantastic scene. Since there was no breeze to blow it away, the gunsmoke hung in the air, mixing with the mist.

The fighting was largely hand-to-hand, and very fierce, but confusing, for almost nobody on either side could be sure by whom he was opposed. The conflict was broken into little groups, especially on the American left, where Coffee rode hard. Everywhere men were getting lost.

At last superior discipline began to tell, and the British rallied and pressed forward. Jackson did something he didn't enjoy—he ordered a retreat.

It was only to be a retreat as far back as the Rodriguez Canal on the Chalmette plantation, behind which Jackson proposed to re-form for another attack.

The British did not pursue. They'd had enough for one night. Besides, it was a common belief among their officers, from Thornton down, that the privates and that sergeant back in the fishing village had not been false; for Jackson, they reasoned must have at least 50,000 men if he threw them in as recklessly as that; and so it would be better to wait until General Keane came up with the main body of the expedition —and a few cannons.

The British, then, posted new pickets, and they went back to their campfires.

Jackson meant to hit them again at dawn, but he was talked out of it. For one thing, the mist had not lifted, and indeed it was worse than before. For another, his Choctaw scouts brought word that the British were being heavily reinforced. So, instead, he dug in, while he ordered up some reinforcements of his own.

The bewilderment of the battle was clear in the figures for the missing, which were uncommonly high. The official killed-wounded-missing figures were: British, 46, 167, and 64; American, 24, 115, and 74. Neither army had been badly mauled; but they were both shaken.

The General was disappointed in this "little Christmas fandango," as he called it; yet in truth, it had been a considerable success, did he but know that. The British had been startled, almost scared, losing some of their cockiness; for they never had supposed that Americans could fight.

The Rodriguez Canal was a man-made irrigation ditch about ten feet wide and three-quarters of a mile long, extending from the river, which fed it, to the swamp, into which it emptied. Because of the lowness of the Mississippi there was no water in the Rodriguez Canal, though the bottom was goo. In itself it was not much of a defense position. The Americans filled it skimpily—for they didn't have many—with caltrops. On the west lip, the side toward the city, they raised a breastwork. There were no rocks in that delta country, and the only trees were in the swamp, from which at least a few branches were taken, as some timber was brought out from New Orleans; but mostly the breastwork was made of dirt and mud, though in a few places bales of cotton were used, these being carefully covered with earth afterward for fear of fire.

It was hard labor for men who had had no sleep, but the General was there to drive them. *He* didn't sleep either.

The British too worked. They already had performed wonders. Their organization was smooth, efficient; and they seemed never to tire. Canoe after canoe was paddled up Bayou Bienvenu, which was too shallow now to permit the use of the landing craft prepared for this purpose. Those fishermen earned their pay! All night this went on, and all the next day.

Andrew Jackson set up his headquarters in the Macarté house a few hundred feet behind the Rodriguez Canal, from the second floor of which house, with a glass, fog permitting, he could survey the whole field.

It had begun to rain again, and was very cold. Where were those blankets? And where were the Kentuckians? Why didn't they arrive? The General sent out an order calling for faster work in the canal defense, and he instructed his engineers to ride to the rear and pick out sites for second and third lines of retreat, in case these should be needed.

The British made no move to attack the next day, Christmas Eve. For one thing, many of them were pinned down behind the levees whenever *Carolina* took it upon herself to hurl a salvo at the camp. For another, though more men were coming up all the time, and the supply machine was functioning without a hitch, still it would be well after dark before the whole force, something immediately in excess of 5,000, would be assembled. They'd be fools to fight before that; and they had no stomach, now, for night attack. A still more telling reason was one that certain outposts on the British side called over to certain outposts on the American side—for there was a great deal of this chitchat, especially in the swamp that protected the British right wing, the American left. These sociable ones revealed that in part the pause was because the vessel bearing the commander-in-chief had arrived off Cat and Ship. When *he* came, they promised, *then* you'd hear things hum! And that would be tomorrow, Christmas Day.

Was it the Duke of Wellington, then? They didn't know. Some said it was, some said no. But the Americans liked to believe that it was, anyway. That would insure a real fight.

Well, they'd learn soon.

Chapter 24

It WAS NOT Wellington—or, as the disrespectful English called him, Dukey. The United States of America was not to be so signally honored, especially at a time when the peace conference at Vienna suggested that there might be war all over again on the continent.

No, not Wellington, but it was the next-best thing, Wellington's own brother-in-law and right-hand man, Major General Sir Edward Packenham.

The newcomer had in his wallet a commission as governor of the Louisiana he would surely conquer. He also had the word of the Regent that when New Orleans had been won he, Packenham, would be awarded an earldom. It was something to fight for.

He was thirty-eight years old, and in perfect health (Jackson was forty-eight, and ill), and he was attended by a large, efficient staff, which included yet another major general, Lambert. Packenham knew, too, that heavy reinforcements were on their way, and that in a few days the size of his force here would be doubled.

He should have been a happy man, and perhaps he was. Reports around the camp said that he had examined the arrangements and the disposition of the troops, and had congratulated General Keane; but other reports asserted that he was as sore as hell, and didn't mind saying so.[42]

Retreat was morally and practically unthinkable. They would be mauled unmercifully if ever they tried to *re*traverse that watery wilderness to the fleet. There was only one way to go—forward.

That was how it seemed to Jackson too, and he watched them, wondering why they didn't come. They seemed to be doing nothing at all, less than a mile and a half away.

As for Jackson himself, he was feverishly busy. Supplies were being brought out from the city, which was searched yet again for every possible firearm, no matter how old, no matter how rusty. Hundreds of Negroes—at one time there were almost 2,000 of them, or as many as there were soldiers manning the line of the Rodriguez Canal—were brought out from New Orleans as laborers. Some of these were free men of color; but they might as well have been slaves. The white residents of New Orleans thought that this applied to them too, the way they were treated. All places of entertainment were shut down. Nobody was allowed to travel between camp and city, either way, without a pass personally signed by the General, who stayed in camp. There was a strict 9 o'clock curfew. Men were tossed into the calaboose on almost any pretext: December 22, the day before the "little Christmas fandango," Mayor Girod had written plaintively to General Jackson that the cells were all filled, and what should they do? What if anything the General replied is not a matter of record; but the arrests continued.

Andrew Jackson was an unaccountable man. When word was brought to him that certain members of the legislature were conspiring to get word to General Packenham offering to make separate peace terms, to surrender the city rather than see it damaged in the damned Yankee cause, he did not, as everybody had expected him to do, blow up. Instead he coldly announced that the legislature was dissolved, and he ordered Governor Claiborne to make an investigation and report back within forty-eight hours. The governor was a hard-working conscientious man, deadly serious, and not likely to minimize anything; and when he reported that there was too little truth in the story for anybody to worry his head about, the General accepted this. The legislature, the General regally said, could function once more. But it is to be doubted that that body ever was the same again.

It rained much of the time, and the nights were cold. Those

men posted along the Rodriguez Canal were mighty uncomfortable. Only the regulars, and not even all of them, had tents. For the rest it was a sleazy blanket—sometimes—and Louisiana mud.

The most uncomfortable of them all was the commander in chief. His dysentery was much worse, and he seldom got more than one hour of sleep at a time. Even his iron will could not endure the pain it brought him to ride, so he hobbled from place to place, always inspecting, always scolding or encouraging, a walking, wincing skeleton. There were many japes about his ailment, but they were told only behind his back.

The British, who were hardly any happier, were less idle than they looked from the Macarté house. It was clear to Packenham that no knockout blow could be struck—save at a horrid cost—so long as those two war vessels hovered off the west bank just opposite the British camp (for *Louisiana,* manned by foreign sailors scraped from the streets of New Orleans, had joined *Carolina*), so he had ordered that four 24-pound howitzers be mounted on the levee, out of reach of the field pieces behind the Rodriguez Canal, but only the width of the river itself, about a mile at that point, from the two vessels. To hull them at that distance would not do much toward silencing them. The best thing was to treat them to hot-shot, and for this reason Packenham had furnaces set up.

On the morning of the 27th these guns opened up on *Carolina* and *Louisiana* alike, and almost immediately one of them scored a spectacular—though probably lucky—hit. There was no trace of breeze, and both vessels floated motionless, each swathed in its own gunsmoke. But soon *Carolina's* guns ceased to bang, and though no fire could be seen from the east shore, men were dropping over her side in a wild scramble, some of them even swimming to safety, so that in a little while she stood deserted. Then she exploded with a roar that rattled windows clear up in New Orleans; and she sank, guns and all, though no men were lost. One of those red-hot balls had penetrated her magazine.

Now all four of the howitzers concentrated on *Louisiana,*

where frantic efforts were being made to get nearer the city, away from the hot-shot. Since there wasn't a cupful of air, this could only be done by means of sweeps and longboats, and there was an excruciating hour while the sloop crawled away, the river around her splattered with geysers from which steam rose. But eventually she made it. She got out of range, taking up another position off the west bank, nearer the city, about opposite the main part of the American encampment, a position from which she could still do a great deal of harm to any advance against the line of the Rodriguez Canal, though she could no longer reach the British camp.

It was a British victory, but only half of the victory it should have been.

Master-Commander Patterson too stayed over on the other side of the river, the west bank, for he took his men from the lost *Carolina* and with them set up a battery of long naval guns just below the place where *Louisiana* now was anchored. These were big guns, and doubtless the site was well selected, but there was no time to emplace them properly and to throw up effective breastworks around them, nor was an arrangement made, in the time that remained, for a falling-back place, a second line. The establishment of this open battery—it was by no stretch of imagination a fort—was the result of General Jackson's fear, a persistent one, that what he faced was only a feint and that the real attack would come elsewhere. He was no longer as touchy about the Chef Menteur road as at first he had been, though he did keep a large force there, and sundry guns; but he feared now that the British might cross the river and outflank him.

On the morning of the 28th General Packenham started an advance in force against the whole Rodriguez line, his army broken into two brigades. It was a splendid sight—there was a touch of sun, for a change—and it must have awed and perhaps even frightened a little the Americans who watched. The kilts of the Scots, the scarlet coats of the infantry, and the green coats of the outflung riflemen—"*They* ain't lobsters!" many a

Tennessean cried—were rigidly massed, exquisitely controlled, coming on without pause, erect, bright, implacable.

The men who lined the bales-of-cotton breastworks, the men with the muskets and rifles—for even officers up to and including the rank of captain carried rifles or muskets—had nothing to do *but* watch and wonder. The British never got near enough to shoot at. It was an artillery show. True, one green-coated company did get too far ahead on the right, near the swamp, so that some Americans leapt the breastwork and the ditch and drove them off; but this was a mere brush.

When the cannons opened up—their range of course was much greater than that of the rifles and muskets—the British didn't waver. They just came right on. Creoles and regulars and ragged men from Tennessee shook their heads, dumfounded. What kind of way was that to act?

The columns were halted, both of them, as men still fell to the ground, here and there. The other soldiers stood motionless while generals conferred, the American guns all the time peppering them with grape. Then they turned, no doubt on command, in perfect order, like wound-up mechanical toys, and, carrying their forty-odd wounded and dead, marched correctly back to camp.

Packenham had learned what he set out to learn. There was a council of war that night, and tempers, the whispers had it, were frayed. Gibbs, a major general, who had commanded the British right wing in the action-no-action of the morning—Jackson in his official report called it a battle, Packenham, in his, a reconnaissance-in-force—was in favor of trying to turn the American left wing, near the swamp, where he said the line was weakest (in fact, that line extended for some distance *into* the swamp, though conceivably General Gibbs did not know this). He argued, additionally, that while the men engaged in such an attack surely would be pounded by the big guns behind the canal, at least they would be out of range of the ones across the river. The firebrand, Admiral Cochrane, was all for dashing right at 'em and slugging it out at close quarters. Were the soldiers reluctant to do this? He offered to bring up the crewmen of his ships, and *they'd* do it.

Packenham, however, was not to be moved. It was a maxim of the military science, he pointed out, that each branch of an army should knock out its corresponding branch in the enemy —the infantry against the infantry, cavalry against cavalry, and so forth—before it can afford to assist some other branch. There was no cavalry on either side in this campaign, and it was up to the artillery to knock out its opposite number before the infantry attacked. Any other method would be appallingly expensive. General Packenham did not wish to start his administration as governor of Louisiana with only a handful of survivors. No, let the guns be massed.

He was the commander-in-chief, and of course he was obeyed.

Chapter 25

THERE WAS NOT the slightest doubt in the British camp that British gunners could outgun Yankee gunners. That much was taken for granted, just as it was taken for granted that, man for man, the British infantry was much superior to that of the United States, given a chance to get in, to come to grips; for the British always had been bayonet specialists. The objection to the immediate knocking-out of the American artillery was only that it would take too much time—time in preparation, that is, not in execution once everything was ready—and time worked on the side of the Americans, for the British plan already was far behind schedule. The Yankees over there were hustling about like ants on an ant heap, staff soldiers pointed out, and if you give that man Jackson time there's no telling how many wild uncouth warriors he might assemble, to make the mopping-up just that much more difficult.

But Packenham said: Emplace those guns.

This would not be easy to do. Never had troopers known such a land! Even in dry weather—if there was such a thing in southern Louisiana—it was all softness underfoot, giving, spongy. There were no rocks. Even to the eye, sometimes, the land seemed to shiver with uncertainty, as though bubbling, as though about to subside into nothingness: this was the appearance of the so-called "quaking prairies" back only a short distance from the river. You couldn't drive piers into ground like that. They'd float away! Why, simply thrust a shovel into it, and the hole you had made was instantly filled with water. How then could you emplace a battery?

The task was made even more formidable by a lack of draft animals. The generals had their mounts, but no pack horses had been brought, for the plan assumed that foragers could fetch these by the score, by the hundred, from surrounding plantations. As it turned out, they couldn't. Jackson or somebody under him—or perhaps it was the planters themselves—had anticipated this; and all livestock had been driven away, so that when the British did come there was not so much as a crippled jackass left to help them. The men had to do all the haulage by means of their own shoulders and backs and arms, moiling in the muck, sweating, swearing.

What's worse, the final emplacement, the bring-up of the guns themselves, the building of defense works, all would have to be done at night, since in the nature of it it must be within range of the American guns, which in daytime could wreak havoc among the emplacers.

The Americans had slave labor. The British had almost none of this—a handful of house servants, a small clump of field hands. They had to do their own work.

The American camp was only a little over five miles from its base, with a good road between. The British camp was eighty-odd miles from *its* base, with no road at all. So even aside from the matter of draft animals, it was infinitely easier for the

Americans to bring up fascines, spades, beams, timber for shoring, not to mention the guns themselves.

Since you couldn't dig down you must build up. Not only did the guns have to be emplaced, but the gunners, in an artillery duel, would have to be protected. And what was there to use for breastworks—or, in the technical term, "epaulements"? The Americans had made gabions, or wickerwork baskets open at both ends, out of branches cut from the cypress swamp. They filled these with mud dredged out of the bottom of the Rodriguez Canal, and stacked them to stop bullets. They called them "cribs." The Americans, after the first tentative try, an emergency measure, used a large number of cotton bales, both for the epaulements around their guns and for their front and rear breastworks. They got three hundred of these from a place even closer and more convenient than the bulging warehouses of New Orleans—the schooner *Pallas*, destined for Havana but held up by the blockade and now anchored in the river near the left bank between camp and city.

Neither of these devices was available to the British. They did make a few gabions of woven cypress limbs, but those limbs came only from the very edge of the swamp, into the depths of which even large parties well protected by troops, and despite the admirable discipline of the British Army, were loath to go. The swamp had a bad name among these invaders. Through it, flitting like shadows, went members of Captain Jugeat's Choctaw company, also the backwoodsmen from Tennessee with their long terrible rifles. You didn't see these men, only felt them when they struck. And then they vanished like smoke. The Choctaws did not collect scalps, for the General had issued an order against this, but like the Tennesseans they would sneak up behind a sentry in the dark and soundlessly cut his throat. It was estimated that about fifty Britishers had been killed in this fashion, a practice that brought about red-faced indignation among Packenham's men, who denounced it as plain murder, their implication being that conventional warfare wasn't.

Of cotton the British had none at all. They did, however,

come upon something they thought would do as well—several hundred hogsheads of sugar stored on the Villeré and Lacoste plantations. They confiscated these, and rolled them out to be ready for the night of emplacement.

That night was the last one of the year 1814. It was dark, starless. It was cold. There was rain again. The soldiers started right after sunset, and the labor was one that might have made Hercules quail.

Despite all injunctions for silence, and the men's most earnest efforts, they were heard. The General was notified: he was of course awake. He nodded, for he had been expecting this. He posted extra sentries, though he was reasonably sure that the British would not attack at night, and he ordered that the whole army be up and at battle stations by three o'clock. If the redcoats came at dawn, in a rush, the Dirty Shirts would be ready for them.

When the dawn did come it was hard to be sure of it, for everything was shrouded in mist and a man couldn't see more than a hundred feet in any direction. Moreover, as that atmosphere makes seeing a bafflement, so too does it distort sound. The men who lined the Rodriguez Canal, though they popped their eyes like tennis balls, and strained their ears, could only make wild guesses as to how many of the enemy were out front and how far away they were. Some swore that the distance was no more than a few yards. (As a matter of record, the closest British guns, the ones nearest to the levee, were only about four hundred yards away. The farthest ones were about half a mile.)

Not until twenty minutes to eleven that New Year's Day morning did the fog lift, and then it did so with an abrupt jerk, with the dramatic gesture of a drawn curtain, revealing a plain crowded with redcoats and their guns.

Almost immediately the British started to fire.

The Americans waited a little while.

The British guns fell into three classes. There were the four 24-pound howitzers that had been mounted on the levee for the purpose of tossing hot-shot at *Louisiana* and *Carolina*.

These were still in position, and they were manned, but they were too far back to be of any effect against the main American guns, though near enough to the river to be within range of Patterson's elevated 18-pounders on the opposite shore, which soon knocked two of them out and brought about the abandonment of the others. There were two field batteries of four 9-pounders each; and there was a siege train made up of ten long 12-pounders.

When they opened up on the American batteries their fire was regular and it was fast. Unaccountably, it was high. Somebody must have miscalculated, somewhere; for all the first balls soared harmlessly over the heads of the American gunners and even over the heads of the reserves.

The British also had a battery of six Congreve rocket tubes, which were slanted toward the American line. These, and the soldiers who manned them, were all a part, if a new part, of the Royal Artillery. Much was expected of them when they were employed against such an enemy as the Americans, who had never seen them before and in many cases never had even heard of them. In the night attack on Fort McHenry at Baltimore, where they were used in America for the first time, they had produced no notable result, save that of a grand fireworks display and the writing of one memorable line of verse, "the rockets' red glare, the bombs bursting in air." But the British hoped that they would be more effective in an open field, in daylight.

The Congreve rocket was designed to be used *in terrorem* rather than for any damage it might happen to inflict, though there was always a chance that one might set something on fire (there was always a chance too that one might fall far short, causing panic in the wrong place, for though considered past the experimental stage they still were exceedingly uncertain in their movements).

The rocket troughs before the Rodriguez line were some distance back, behind the siege guns. They were manned by 200 specially trained artillerists.

A 32-pound Congreve rocket—such as these were—consisted

of a 3½-foot metal head fastened to a 15-foot wooden guiding stick. It was packed with black powder and fitted with a time fuse. It carried the stick along with it when it was fired. They made a great deal of noise and sent out columns of intimidating black smoke, but they seldom did any real harm. On the plain at Chalmette they didn't scare the Americans at all, for most of them, like most of the early balls, went much too high.

Opposing this armament the Americans had a heterogeneous collection of cannons that was technically superior to the British, at least in the amount of metal it could throw, but actually, because it consisted of six different types of gun with five different calibers, could be expected to be weaker. There were an iron 32-pound carronade, which had a terrific recoil but wouldn't carry far; three long iron 24-pounders; one Spanish long brass 18-pounder; one U.S. Navy long iron 18-pounder; three French brass 12-pounders; six American brass 6-pounders; and one 10-inch mortar.

The mortar had been brought along only in the hope that somebody could be found who knew how to fire it, for there were no time fuses for its shells, useless elsewhere. It had not been used in the night battle of the 23rd, nor yet at the time of Packenham's reconnaissance-in-force. A few days ago, however, somebody had turned up with a French army veteran named Jules Lefebre, who knew all about these weapons, even how to make time fuses for them; and now he was busily at work. Yet at that distance the mortar could hardly be expected to do much damage, while the 6-pounders were of no use at all.

Patterson's guns across the river could not reach the British batteries on the plain, only the howitzers.

The American artillery took its time, as a cool duelist might have done. Not for a quarter-hour, the while the British guns boomed furiously, did the Americans really shoot; and even when they did open fire it was slowly, as though not sure of themselves, a circumstance that heartened the British gunners.

Those British gunners had very early spotted the Macarté mansion, a large two-story white wooden building, and no doubt they deduced that it was General Jackson's headquarters, for they poured an intense fire into it: seventy hits were counted, later. They were wasting their time. Jackson, with all his staff, was at the front line.

Soon the American fire quickened and became more regular, and from the beginning it had proved to be most marvelously accurate. It concentrated on the siege guns, the 12-pounders, and soon had five of these out of action.

"Meantime we could not see that we had silenced so much as one of their guns; and their fire grew more and more accurate with every discharge," testified the acting chief of artillery on the British side.[43] "The battery of theirs that did us by far the most injury was the third one from their right which brought it about opposite to the centre of our formation."

This was the battery of two long 24-pounders manned by the Baratarians, thirty-six bushy-bearded scarlet-shirted ruffians under the command of the redoubtable Dominick You. Their *bos,* Jean Lafitte, was not there.

The British suffered even more in manpower, and that for two reasons. They were massed closer, there being some 4,000 of them besides the gunners, ready for a charge when, as was fully expected, the American guns had been silenced; and their protection was weaker.

The cotton-bale defenses were proving a failure. They could stop a bullet—though none were flying today anyway—and they could even stop a fair-sized ball; but they caught fire too readily; and when, as sometimes did happen, a Congreve, falling short, landed on one of these bales—then there was trouble for everybody nearby. The flames were not great, but the smoke was. Thick and black, it stung the eyes, blurring vision. The gunners, when these bales were knocked out of place and ignited all around them, cursed the things and went right on working their guns, but the men along the front line in many places toppled the burning bales into the canal, where, hissing and spluttering in the slime, they sent up more smoke than ever.

The British with their hogsheads of sugar were even more unfortunate. American balls tore those hogsheads open, or so cracked them that the thin malicious rain got at their contents, melting these. Splinters were flying, always a danger, as seamen knew. Gun after gun, badly protected, was dismounted; and soldier after soldier, half-crazed with cold and hunger—they had been fed only a few ship's biscuits and a tot of rum since sunset of the previous day, and some had not even had this much, for all carriage power must be used to bring up the guns, the hogsheads, and the ammunition—tried to eat the sugar thus exposed. They found it quite different from the trim white crystalline loaf sugar they had known at home. It was thick sticky black stuff, unrefined, full of grit and little splinters of cane. In every case it made them violently sick.

Fortunately they were not called upon to fight, those vomiting ones, for after a conference with his aides General Packenham agreed that the artillery duel had been a complete, unmitigated, and astounding failure, and he ordered a retreat.

Now Cochrane and Gibbs and the others could not be answered. Clearly the only thing to do was smash these unorthodox Americans right in the middle; and Packenham began to make preparations accordingly.

Chapter 26

THE NATION WAITED on tiptoe for news from New Orleans. That the country was about to be invaded again, and in greater force than ever, was generally known, though details were lacking, in east and west alike, but most emphatically in the east, since because of the British blockade all communications had to be by land, across the mountains.

The outlook was gloomy. Pessimism was the order of the day. The country teetered on the edge of bankruptcy, Washington lay in ruins, no welcome word could be expected from Europe. For all practical purposes there was no navy left; and the least said about the army the better. Goods rotted in warehouses, while ships rotted in port. The American people no longer had any confidence in their political *or* their military leaders.

"The ship of state has gone aground," was the general belief, outspoken everywhere in New England, not altogether unvoiced elsewhere.

If the news from Louisiana proved to be bad, as almost certainly it would, then the country would fall apart. There might be some wry enjoyment in speculating on how the split would form itself—whether New York would go out with New England, perhaps New Jersey and Pennsylvania as well; whether the South and West would cling together; in other words, would the country break into two parts, three parts, or four? After the burning of the Capitol, after everything else, James Madison simply would be forced to resign when it was learned that New Orleans had fallen.[44]

Few hopes could be held out for the peace conference at Ghent. Why should the British agree even to treat, when they had the upper hand? That a castle that consents to parley, like a woman who consents to listen, already is half won—this was not remembered. The circumstance that the five-man United States delegation was superior in every way to the three-man English delegation, like the circumstance that diplomatic Great Britain was too deeply immersed in the Congress of Vienna to pay much attention to this side show in the Low Countries, was not known to the average citizen. Except for the appointment of the delegates and the Senate's confirmation of these, there was only one piece of news given to the public about the proceedings at Ghent, though admittedly this was an important one: the initial British terms, set forth in August at Ghent, received at Washington and by Washington published late in October.

These terms were not harsh, considering that Great Britain was by so much the stronger nation, considering also that such terms when first advanced traditionally are more than the advancer expects to win; but the American public didn't reason that way, and the cry of rage was loud.

The cry of rage in England, at least in official circles, was equally loud. Publication of diplomatic papers before the consummation of any treaty or formal agreement simply wasn't done. It was a dirty Yankee political trick; and if President Madison at about this time [45] had not instructed the American delegates no longer to hold out for renunciation of the principle of impressment as a *sine qua non,* the negotiations might have broken down then and there.

"Have you attended to the solemn and almost unanimous declaration of the legislature of Connecticut?" Stockton of New Jersey asked the House of Representatives. "Have you examined the cloud arising in the East? Do you perceive that it is black, alarming, portentous?"

He was referring to the so-called Hartford Convention, to be opened December 15. Everybody knew that the convention had been called by Federalists for the purpose of discussing secession, and that the government was powerless to block or prevent it. That the delegates to this convention, one and all, were conservative men and not likely to do anything rash [46] only made the matter seem more certain. That the convention sessions would be secret sounded ominous—though the Congressional sessions that decided upon war had been secret, all of them, as had the four-day session of the Second Continental Congress that debated and adopted the Declaration of Independence. James Monroe spoke in his capacity as Secretary of War rather than that of Secretary of State when he ordered Major Jessup, who was stationed in Hartford at the time, trying to recruit for the 25th U.S. Infantry, to keep an eye on the meetings and to report directly to him, Monroe.

Still, it was thought that the Hartford sages would not need to take an irrevocable step, since the nation was sure to fall apart at news of the loss of New Orleans anyway.

With all of this Andrew Jackson had nothing to do, and his confidence never wavered, he was too busy.

The artillery duel of January 1 pleased him. They had cap-

tured five large cannons, guns damaged beyond repair, to be
sure, but still useful as trophies,[47] and they had lost none of
their own. They had learned that baled cotton is no good for
breastworks, and they'd hauled all this to the rear, where it was
dumped, and where shivering soldiers ripped it to pieces to
stuff it under their uniforms and to make beds of it. Best of
all, the men had not flinched.

"It [the bombardment] was sustained by every corps under
my command with a firmness which would have done honor
to veterans," the General wrote to Monroe next day. But he
added: "P.S. no news from the Kentucky Troops, no arms, ammunition or equipments has arrived."

The following day he wrote the same thing about the lack
of supplies or reinforcements. And—where ever were those
5,000 blankets?

The day after *that* the Kentuckians started to dribble into
New Orleans in rafts and keelboats of one sort and another,
tired, disheveled men, not a quarter of whom had guns. "I
don't believe it," the General cried. "I never met a man from
Kentucky yet but he had a bottle of whiskey, a deck of cards,
and a gun." Nevertheless it was true, as he learned when they
straggled out to the camp. Kentucky had so stripped herself of
firearms for the various campaigns in the northwest that there
were virtually none left. The assumption of the governor—like
that of Blount when he dispatched the second division of Tennessee militia south—had been that there was a large store of
arms and ammunition in New Orleans, and that all he needed
to send Jackson was men.

Once again the city was scoured, and a few ancient muskets
were passed out; but for the most part the Kentuckians had
nothing but their hunting knives.

The General hobbled back and forth, scowling. What was the
matter with those rascals out there? Hadn't they learned *yet,*
by the Eternal, that the lies he had caused to be spread about
his strength were exactly that, and that he didn't have even
as many men as they did? Why didn't they strike?

A deputation of merchants from New Orleans came calling

at the Macarté house. They didn't demand—for they had learned that you don't demand things of Andrew Jackson—but they respectfully if with an irksome persistence asked whether if the General had to retreat through the city he would burn it, as the Russians had burned Moscow. It was, understandably, important for them to know this.

The General didn't fly into a rage. He scarcely appeared to hear them, even after they had repeated the question several times. At last he said that he had no answer to give, and he dismissed them.

It is likely that he had not made up his own mind. And why should he? Backward was a direction in which he was not accustomed to go. Besides, he was much more interested in the British. *Why* didn't they come?

They did come, January 8.

Chapter 27

IT WAS NOT cowardice that held the British back. Heaven forbid. Nor were they any longer unaware of the size of Jackson's army, which now numbered only slightly more than their own, though it was not concentrated, as theirs was, for Jackson had large bodies probing every possible bayou by which he might be flanked, and kept also a large force, three whole regiments, guarding the Chef Menteur road.

Jackson of course had been strengthening his defense works all the while, but there wasn't much else he could do. He was twitchy, himself. He kept going around the camp, saying words of encouragement, from time to time glaring out across the plain to where the British lay. He feared that he would be caught in another trap, his professional ignorance exposed. A pitched fight—that was one thing. But he wasn't much of a man with a map.

That was a terrible week, a week of strain and sweat. And the weather went right on being bad.

It was not a happy time for the British either. Thornton on December 23 had not ventured to advance upon New Orleans, though there was no defense in sight then. Packenham on the 28th had taken a massive look—and returned to camp. How, then, could they hope to succeed January 8?

There were two reasons: (1) another heavy reinforcement, some 3,000 men under Major General Lambert, was due any day; and (2) Packenham and his officers at last had worked out a plan for flanking the American right.

As a matter of military sense, if not of humanity, no general likes to lose a lot of men at one time. The artillery duel had been a resounding failure, nor could it be tried again with what was left. Flanking the American left, deep into the swamp, was out of the question. With their heavy equipment the troops would be bogged down—if they could be persuaded to go there in the first place. At the tip of their right wing the Americans had built a flèche or arrowhead-shaped breastwork open at the back, right on the inner levee, some distance forward of the Rodriguez Canal, and this, with some riflemen and a couple of field guns, would make a turning movement there expensive if not impossible. To go farther around the American right would mean crossing the river, where Patterson's troublesome battery might be taken and used against the Americans just before a frontal rush was launched. But—how to get across?

It was at this point that peppery little Admiral Cochrane came forth with a plan suggested to him, he said, by his own engineers, who, he was convinced, were brighter than the Army engineers.

The Villeré Canal was another of the drainage ditches common in those parts, stretching between river and swamp, or, in the case of this one, Bayou Mazant, a branch of Bayou Bienvenu. It passed right through the British camp, and like the others it was shallow and presently without water, though its bottom was mud.

Cochrane proposed to deepen this its whole length, more than a mile, and then haul or float into it a large number of ships' boats ready and waiting on Lake Borgne, the same boats that would bring Lambert's men forward. The levee could be breached for this purpose: there was no danger of a flood, with the river this low. Then, once the boats were in the canal, a dam could be built at the swamp end of the canal to prevent the water that was coming in from the river from escaping into Bayou Mazant, and this would raise the water level in the Villeré Canal, so that the boats could be floated right out upon the river itself.

Colonel Thornton, that salamander, would be given charge of the flanking force—the 5th West India regiment, the 85th regulars, 200 seamen, 200 marines, in all about 1,200 rank and file.

They would cross the river in this fashion, making never a sound, the night of January 7. They would march upon Patterson's rickety "fort," built around an old lime kiln, surprise it, take it, and then take Patterson's battery just above it. This would be a little before dawn, January 8. At a signal from Packenham, on the east bank, Patterson's own captured guns would open up on the Rodriguez line and the American camp. At the same time, six 18-pounders, to be remounted on the east bank about 800 yards from the Rodriguez Canal, would do the same. After a brief but vigorous bombardment from two directions, the east-bank force would make a frontal attack, while Lambert moved up a reserve consisting of the 43rd and the fusileers, about 1,200 more men.

It was a superb plan, on paper. But it called for an enormous amount of heavy work—most of which would have to be done at night, since if Jackson saw it and guessed its purpose he could enlarge and make alert the force defending the Patterson battery so that no surprise would be possible—and this on the part of men weakened, all but exhausted, their ranks thinned by sickness (the British hospital was full to the last cot, and still they came in: the hospital was just below headquarters, which itself was just below the Villeré Canal). Moreover, it involved almost split-minute co-ordination between two large bodies of men on opposite sides of a mile-wide river, bodies that had no means of communicating with one another except for the start-in rocket that Packenham would fire.

An essential of the plan was that Thornton move all his men, and get them over there, before the first peep of dawn; for if they were discovered by daylight anywhere on the face of the stream they could be slaughtered by Patterson's guns on the far shore or by the 6-pounders mounted in the flèche on the levee or even by the *Louisiana*. (It happened that *Louisiana*, anchored on the west bank just above Patterson's battery, was manned only by a maintenance crew, all her gunners having been sent ashore to help the sailing-commander; but the British didn't know this; and it hardly mattered anyway.)

Lambert arrived with his men the 6th. The work on the Villeré Canal had appeared to go well, and ships' boats were clustered in the swamp ready for the push, the crossing. It was believed that Jackson suspected nothing.

Nor did he. But on that same day the opening of the levee, the deepening of the canal, the assembling of ships' boats, was spotted by some sharp-eyed tar with a glass, across the river on a *Louisiana* cross-tree. Patterson sent word to the General.

It didn't arrive until the following day, the 7th. Jackson did not take it very seriously. He still kept scouting parties poking into all the bayous north and northeast of the city, and he refused to withdraw the three regiments on the Chef Menteur road. Patterson on the far shore had besides his own naval gunners and a couple of hundred Negro laborers, some 450 members of the Louisiana militia under General Morgan. That should be enough for him. However, there were all those Kentuckians milling around, getting in the way; so he sent 400 of these across to the west bank. No provision had been made for moving troops either way across the river at that point, and these had to be marched five miles to New Orleans, where they were supposed to collect their guns, muskets hidden to the last aching moment in fear of a slave uprising, and only recently dug up. Then they should cross on the ferry and march down to Patterson's camp. They did this, but fewer than half of them got there, early on the morning of January 8, and those were staggering from weariness, half-starved, and by no means all armed, for the roundup of old fowling pieces at New Orleans had been less successful than reported.

British engineers had not taken the nature of the delta country soil sufficiently into account. The Villeré Canal was deepened and water did ooze in, the dam was built, the breach was made in the levee, but—the walls kept caving in. Forty-seven longboats had been brought into the canal, enough to carry over Thornton's force of 1,200, but they were not actually afloat, rather they rested on mud. The gates at the river were opened, but the dam at the other end wasn't capable of holding the rush of water, and it broke. This and the unstable walls put the boats on mud again. Rollers weren't available, and probably would not have worked if they were. The boats had to be hauled, had to be *shoved* through the slime.

The rendezvous was to have been at nine. Thornton was there, and all the men attached to him, but there were no boats. The colonel waited . . . and waited. Not until almost 1 o'clock in the morning did boats begin to appear, a straggling line of them. But not many came.

Everything depended upon Thornton, who was already, through no fault of his own, more than four hours late. He had hesitated on the 23rd. He did not hesitate tonight. To send to headquarters for instructions would take too long. He picked about 400 of the best men, and at the head of these, with muffled thole pins, he pushed off.

The field guns had been brought up and re-emplaced, and though the epaulements were flimsy it was not expected that this would be a long bombardment, only a preliminary cover for the troops.

The men were brought silently into position, a little before 4 o'clock. Gibbs on the right, Keane on the left, Lambert in the rear.

The foremost riflemen, skirmishers, were within 150 yards of the Rodriguez Canal, though there was nothing to indicate that their presence was known by the Americans. The reserve itself was only about 700 yards back.

Everything was committed. Gibbs had the 4th, 21st, 44th, and three companies of the 95th, about 2,200 in all. Keane on the left had the 93rd, two companies of the 95th, two companies of the fusileers, and the 43rd, about 1,200 rank and file. The reserve numbered close to 2,000.

There were about 5,300 men all told, plus officers and sergeants.

Scaling ladders had been distributed. Fascines had been made out of great bundles of green sugar cane: they were heavy, and awkward to handle, but the men wouldn't have to tote them far before dumping them into the Rodriguez Canal. Roughly, one quarter of the men in each forward outfit were supposed to be carrying fascines or ladders.

At the last moment something went wrong. It was learned that the 44th, on the right, where the main attack was to be made, had gone forward without its fascines and scaling ladders. Seconds were precious now, for it was 5 o'clock, and despite the mist the Americans might at any moment see this host in their front yard and open up on it.

Packenham sent an officer forward, then went forward himself. The officer, returning, reported that Lieutenant Colonel Mullens, in charge of the 44th,[48] had paused at the redan where his men's ladders and fascines were stocked, but had received no instructions and met no officer of engineers, and so had gone on to the front. He and his men had been ordered back to that redan, 600 yards over foot-cutting stubble, at a run. Mullens didn't like this, nor did the men, who muttered that they were being used as cannon fodder, that they had been assigned to the suicide flank.

But apparently everything was all right now, at a little after 5. General Packenham started to raise his arm to give the signal for the rocket.

Then an aide came to tell him about Thornton, and about

the delay there. Thornton couldn't possibly seize those batteries and turn them against the American camp before the break of dawn. But, the aide pointed out, there was still time to withdraw the troops before they were seen in the spreading daylight.

General Packenham shook his head.

"I have deferred the attack twice already," he said. "Fire that rocket."

Chapter 28

THAT ROCKET CAUSED no consternation among the Americans, who, wrapped in fog through which their fires gleamed wanly, were having breakfast. In most cases this consisted of corn bread and whiskey. The complaint among the Creoles was about the absence of coffee, a prized possession since the blockade. There was a little. Despite all regulations, certain New Orleans relatives and friends had managed to get a bit of coffee to certain friends and relatives in camp. At Battery 3, where the General, making his rounds, paused to have a cup with Dominick You, there was very good coffee indeed. The General smacked his lips.

"Best I ever tasted. Where'd you get it? Smuggled it, I suppose?"

The Baratarian only grinned.

Nor did anybody there cry in astonishment when the mist rolled away, and the sun lazily rose, to reveal the British army drawn up in two columns, the middle of the field being empty except for the guns in back. This too they had expected, and they were ready for it, their guns loaded.

The band started to play, loudly.

The people of New Orleans loved music in any form, and the municipal band, made up of amateurs, was often called to the Place d'Armes.[49] It had been brought out to the camp a week ago, to play at a New Year's Day celebration planned to hearten the troops—a celebration that had to be postponed because of the artillery duel. The band had remained, and now it was in action again.

This was Sunday, but it was not hymns that the band played: it was "Yankee Doodle."

The British guns banged, and immediately afterward the American guns. This sound—the guns, not the band—was easily heard on the other side of the river; and Patterson's long heavy 18-pounders started to speak, firing not at the American camp but at the advancing British column nearer the levee.

Thornton, then, had not made it.

(Because he had not allowed for the current, Thornton landed two miles below the designated place, and just now he wasn't anywhere near Patterson's battery, which, too late, he was to take.)

Redcoats began to drop. Some slammed backward as though clubbed; some simply crumbled; and some slipped to their knees, swayed a moment as though in prayer, and then toppled. Their companions in the ranks, bayonets fixed, stepped delicately past them. The order was: never let yourself be flustered by a bloody corpse, but act as if it wasn't there.

Stone-faced, the British went on.

This amazed the men who lined the Rodriguez Canal. They were packed close, about 3,200 of them, as many as the half-mile line would hold. On the extreme right, manning the flèche, were the blue-shirted members of Beale's Rifles. Next to them were the 7th regular infantry, not veterans but on the contrary raw youths who never before had been under fire. Then Plauché's gaily caparisoned battalion, the pride of New Orleans. Then LaCoste's Santo Domingans and Daquin's free men of color. Then the 44th, as inexperienced an outfit as the 7th. The rest of the line was largely made up of Tennessee militia, the General's own, first Carroll's, then Coffee's men stretching along an extension of the breastwork into the swamp. There was, however, an indeterminate force of Kentuckians, all armed, between these two Tennessee regiments, put there at the last minute, and it was toward this spot that Gibbs's men appeared to be converging. Most of the Kentuckians were in the rear. They had only their tomahawks and hunting knives, but if worse came to worst they could grab firearms from fallen men and fight a retreating action.

There was no rifle or musket fire at first. The men along the line had been told to wait until they were sure that their guns would reach, and then to aim at the place just above where the crossbelts crossed, a perfect target. So they waited. The redcoats who were falling were falling because of artillery fire.

This was round shot from the other side of the river, for grape would not have reached that far. It was largely grape, however, from behind the Rodriguez Canal, where most of the batteries had used up all their round shot in the New Year's Day duel.

Gibbs obliqued, making for the Kentuckians. Soon his men came within small arms range, and then Kentuckians and Tennesseans alike fired.

Nothing like it ever had been known before. These men did not fire in volleys, as members of any civilized European army would have done, but each for himself. They were close-packed, and they were wondrously quick to reload. It was not the usual crackle of musketry and rifle fire: it was almost one continuous roar, one great sheet of flame.

Redcoats no longer dropped just here and there, now and then. Rather they fell in swaths, as though cut down by some gigantic scythe. Here was Breed's Hill all over again, forty years later.

It was too much. Gibbs's column broke, nobody having reached the canal. It is a measure of the terror these men felt that they ran for the nearest cover, the dreaded swamp.

Keane knew a moment of success when his second-in-command, young Colonel Rennie, led a charge against the flèche—

and took it. Beale's Rifles rallied, however, and with the aid of the adjacent 7th infantry they organized a countercharge, driving the British out. Rennie, with others, was killed.

It all happened quickly, and the band never ceased to play.

Keane saw that across the field Gibbs was having trouble trying to rally his men—he never did manage to rally the 44th, Mullens' regiment, which had given in completely to panic, but he did bring parts of the 4th and the 21st out of the swamp—and so of his own accord, without orders, Keane dispatched the 93rd to Gibbs's assistance.

This was a Highland regiment, indeed "the most Highland of the Highland regiments," the Sutherlanders, and the men wore the full colorful garb of their ancestors, with leathered bonnets, the kilt and plaid being of the Sutherland tartan, a sett dark and predominantly green. It was a crack outfit, and exceptionally large, 900 rank and file.

It started straight across the field, its left side turned to the men behind the breastwork, but when it came within range of the Tennessee rifles a strange thing happened. The whole regiment stopped dead. The men could have been frozen with fear; but this is not likely. It is more probable that somebody got orders confused, and the men waited in doglike obedience to be told what to do. At any rate the Scots simply stood there—though they did not stand long. As had happened with the 44th, farther to the right, they were cut down in swaths. When at last they recovered their nerve, or the proper order at last was given, only *one hundred and sixty* were left of the 900 to stumble to the rear.

Within a few minutes of the opening of the rifle and musket fire there wasn't a mounted officer in sight. General Keane was shot off his horse and had to be carried from the field, badly wounded.

Soon afterward, Gibbs, still striving to rally his men, was hit four times together, any one of which balls would have been fatal. He was cursing horribly when he fell, and he continued to curse until he died, like a real soldier.

A few men got into the Rodriguez Canal, but they were without ladders, as they were without support, and they made no try to scale the wall, but only clung to it, below the line of fire. One man only, a major, topped the breastwork—to fall dead on the other side.

Major General Sir Edward Packenham, seeing that Gibbs was in trouble, rode forward to help him. Now the Americans loved mounted men, who must be officers. Packenham was shot in the left forearm. His horse was killed underneath him, but he borrowed another and started to ride on. A bullet in the neck brought him to earth again, and as his aides clustered about him a piece of grape tore open his thigh, smashing a blood vessel.

Packenham would never be governor of Louisiana. He would never be an earl, now.[50]

His last words were an order to Lambert, the only remaining general, to bring up the reserves. But Lambert had better sense. Heroism aside, the day, definitely, was lost. This wasn't a battle, it was butchery! You couldn't even tell the color of the earth for the soldiers that lay upon it, a blanket of scarlet and of the Sutherland green. There were more than 3,000 of them.

Lambert ordered a retreat.

The band ceased playing "Yankee Doodle" and swung into "Hail Columbia."

The American losses were 8 killed, 13 wounded. Two-thirds of the men behind the Rodriguez line never had been given a chance to fire a shot.

Almost immediately, and despite shouted orders, these men began to climb over the breastwork and to cross the canal and cruise among the fallen. As a result of this there were some incidents. For example, one officer, prone, pistoled a man who approached him—and was promptly done in by indignant Tennesseans. That officer and others like him misunderstood. The Americans were not scurrying around the field in order to cut throats or to take scalps, as Indians would have done. A few went out to see if they could help the wounded; but most of them were simply looking for souvenirs.

Chapter 29

A GOOD GENERAL is one who wins battles, and the more battles he wins the better general he is. A poor general is a general who does not win battles. It's as simple as that. War is mankind's most egregious folly, yet it pretends to be practical. "What counts," aver the strategists, from the depths of their armchairs, "is results."

Jackson did not pursue the British or do anything to annoy them in the course of their retreat to their ships, a masterfully executed movement. He preferred to stay behind his parapets, and no doubt he was wise in this, for though the British lion had had its snout rubbed into the dirt it had plenty of bite left. Jackson had done all he needed to do, much more than anybody ever had expected him to do, when he stemmed the red tide. Motionless, he was a hero.

He was a most stupendous hero, and swiftly became known all over the country as, simply, *The* Hero. The American public had needed him.

Flamboyance is of the essence of New Orleans. This battle has been tooted and decorated and swagged with superlatives more than most, and it will continue to be. Nevertheless, and though we do not have to accept without challenge the rating given it by one of its most distinguished narrators, Judge Walker, who found that it was "the most brilliant victory . . . since the invention of gunpowder," [51] undeniably it was a first-class show. If it settled nothing, neither did the war. Andrew Jackson had made almost every mistake it was possible to make, but he did the last thing right—he won—and nothing else mattered.

Two days before the battle, the Federalists in Hartford adjourned "without day," and it became evident that New England wasn't about to split with the rest of the nation just yet. The relief was heady. A mountain had labored and brought forth a mouse, the waggish cried; though in Boston most folks preferred to quote this in the original Horace: *Parturiunt montes, nascetur ridiculus mus.*

The day after the "little Christmas fandango"—that is, December 24, 1814—three Englishmen and five Americans at Ghent signed a treaty. It had been a near thing for a while, but the pressure for peace put upon the Britishers eventually told; and once Great Britain had surrendered the principle of *uti possidetis* the thing was done; for nobody wanted to go on anyway; and out of that diplomatic muck-and-moil there emerged a settlement on the basis of *status quo ante,* which is to say that everybody was back where he had started from, only poorer.

True, there wasn't a word in the treaty [52] about the two reasons the United States had given for declaring war in the first place, the orders-in-council and the impressment of seamen; but—who cared?

The news of the treaty of peace and the news of the battle of New Orleans reached most parts of the country at about the same time, and the joy they produced verged on hysteria.

Except in humiliation, as wars go it had not been expensive, for it cost the country only about $127 million and 5,000 lives, that latter figure being less than a third of the losses in any one of the larger Civil War *battles.*

It is wrong to say that the battle of New Orleans, fought two weeks after peace had been declared, gained nothing and proved nothing. It gave us a hero; and though he may be not much more than a myth today, Andrew Jackson, for all his cantankerousness and for all his narrowness of mind, radically changed the history of the United States of America. Perhaps this alone made the whole thing worth while.

Notes

1. The word is a corruption of the Spanish *cimarron,* "wild," "untamed," and has no connection with the color, which was named after the chestnut. The verb, "to maroon," meaning to cast upon a small island to die, a common punishment among pirates and buccaneers of the West Indies, is also from *cimarron.*

2. There were certain skippers who in the name of smartness ordered that every time the topmen were piped down, the last to hit the deck—he probably had been the first to go aloft and hence one of the best—should get ten lashes, or twenty, or thirty. This resulted in a great many broken ankles and even some deaths because of the mad scramble at the last moment. "Smartness" was a fetish. On some warships everything was done at the double—everything topside, that is—and everything was scrubbed three times, whether or not it needed scrubbing. The Duke of Wellington was reported to have said after being taken over such a ship, yes, everything was bright—"except the faces of the men." The literature on the misery of life in the British Navy of that time is immense. A few items are included in the *Sources;* see Masefield, Wetherell, Durand, Hutchinson.

3. Jefferson's party, still so new, the first in the country, was in complete command, the Federalists being a slim minority in New England, New York, and Maryland. The Jeffersonian group at this time was called, customarily, the Republican party, though sometimes it was called the democratic party, with a small "d." Soon afterward it came to be known as the Republican-Democratic party or the Democratic-Republican party, indifferently, by those who liked as by those who hated

it; and in time it came to be called simply the Democratic party. The Republican party as we know it today was not organized until 1856.

4. Parsons, *Jean Lafitte,* pp. 3-4. The original, dated February 19, 1813, is in the Bibliotheca Parsoniana, New Orleans.

5. The big cleavage came later, and was to last at least until the invention of talking movies. True, the Reverend John Witherspoon, president of Princeton, already had commented upon the looseness of grammar in the new states, at that time (1781) coining the word "Americanism," and the first of Noah Webster's dictionaries, which were to point up the differences of talk on the two sides of the Atlantic, was published in 1806. Nevertheless an Englishman then would have judged an American's talk not as vulgar so much as old-fashioned, rather quaint. See M. M. Mathews, *The Beginnings of American English* (University of Chicago Press, 1931), also H. L. Mencken's *The American Language* (4th edition, Knopf, 1936), together with *Supplement I* (1945) and *Supplement II* (1948).

6. *The Doctrine of Continuous Voyage* by Charles Burke Elliott, *American Journal of International Law,* vol. I, part I, pp. 61-104. It was based on the so-called Rule of 1756, and Elliott calls it, bluntly, a law designed to cripple American commerce, which of course it' was. The American answer to it was the Doctrine of Broken Voyage, by which a U.S. vessel could pick up in the French West Indies a cargo of, say, sugar; then, instead of making directly for France with this, it could take it to an American port, unload, and load another cargo which, oddly enough, might turn out to be sugar; and with *this* cargo, and fresh papers, go to France and a big profit, secure against British interference. This raised a howl in England and prompted the publication of an immensely popular book, *War in Disguise,* by James Stephens. That title "war in disguise" was on every islander's lips, and it was spoken bitterly, very much as today we refer to the cold war. See also Carr, *The Coming of War,* part 4, chapter 3. The British made sundry spirited if not wholly successful efforts to smash the

Doctrine of Broken Voyage, causing even more hard feeling. The matter never was settled, not even by war.

7. "It could at least be said for France that the diplomatic blundering of Napoleon was opposed by his ministers to the limited extent of their daring. The British government had perfect teamwork in perversity." Brant, *James Madison*, Vol. V, p. 483.

8. A not inconsiderable mêlée-among-the-professors in regard not to the activities but to the motivation of the War Hawks has sprung up lately in certain learned publications. See, in *Sources,* Pratt, Anderson, Cady, Coleman, Goodman, Hacker, Lewis, Smith, Taylor. The most recent book on the subject— and an excellent one—is Carr's *The Coming of War: An Account of the Remarkable Events Leading to the War of 1812.*

9. It should be pointed out that Randolph of Roanoke was not at this time the power that he had been and was to be again in Congress. An irascible, a scolding, scalding, poly-syllabic Virginian, he could hardly be claimed by either party, for he had made a career of opposition, and was a party in himself; so much so that the compiler of the Annals of Congress, in which the names of Federalist members were printed in roman type while those of Republicans were printed in italics, solved his dilemma by printing John Randolph's name in *both* types, alternating them. Randolph could be a delight in personal conversation, but on the floor he sometimes became inebriated with the exuberance of his own verbosity; and the wonder was that he kept away from the dueling strip as long as he did. It was Henry Clay, then an *ex*-War Hawk, and Secretary of State under John Quincy Adams, who finally did call him out—and get him there. In the Senate Randolph had referred to Clay as a "blackleg," and had expressed pity that Clay's forebears had produced "this being so brilliant yet so corrupt, which, like a rotten mackerel by moonlight, shined and stunk." The challenge followed. Randolph accepted it, though he protested that he could not legally or morally be

summoned to the field of honor by reason of words spoken in debate, and announced that he did not believe he had a right to shoot at Mr. Clay, and would not do so, though Mr. Clay had a right to shoot at him, once he had waived his Congressional immunity. This distinction earned Randolph much praise. Its tickle niceness charmed even those who abhorred him. The two met the afternoon of Saturday, April 8, 1826, on the Virginia side of the Potomac above the bridge at Little Falls. The terms were the customary ones, smooth-bore pistols at ten paces. The Senator—it was so like him!—made his appearance wearing a white flannel dressing robe and bedroom slippers. He fired into the air. Clay's bullet punctured the dressing robe but not the man inside it. Randolph offered to call quits. "Tut —this is mere child's play," cried the Secretary of State. "I insist on another shot." So they did it again, with exactly the same result. Then they shook hands. "You owe me a coat, Mr. Clay," the Senator said. "I am glad the debt is no greater," cried the Secretary of State. Two days later, on the Monday, they exchanged cards, making known to the world that they were friends again. It was all very gentlemanly. Adams, pp. 286-7; Stevens, pp. 212-9; Schurz, pp. 273-5. Thomas Hart Benton, surely a connoisseur of such affairs, thought it "about the last high-toned duel that I have witnessed, and among the most high-toned that I have ever witnessed." *Thirty Years' View*, Vol. I, p. 77.

10. Appendix B.

11. It has been said that though figures don't lie liars figure. Some of the figures in the impressment controversy are fantastic, and the matter will probably never be straightened. For the report of the Massachusetts House of Representatives committee see Channing, *History*, Vol. IV, pp. 481-83, and Zimmerman, *Impressment*, pp. 259-275. Guesses on the part of perfervid patriots as to the number of American seamen serving perforce in the British Navy ranged all the way up to 50,000. On the other hand, at just about the time that the Massachusetts House committee was hearing its witnesses, Castlereagh

told the Commons that of 145,000 men in the Royal Navy only 800 claimed American birth. Adams, *History*, Vol. VII, p. 19.

12. There is an extensive literature about William Hull and his trial. Two of the fairest and most readily accessible accounts—especially interesting since the first tends to defend while the other condemns the General—are to be found in Adams, *History*, Vols. VI and VII, and Mahan, *Sea Power*, Vol. I, pp. 347-50.

13. The Society of St. Tammany is no new thing! It was founded May 12, 1789, just two weeks after the federal government itself came into being, and like the federal government it has been operating ever since. Myers, *History*, passim; Werner, *Tammany Hall;* Alexander, *Political History*, Vol. I, p. 181. Tammanyites of the time often were called Martling Men, after the hall in which they met; but the society was the same.

14. Fortescue, *British Army,* Vol. X, p. 105.

15. The use of "sloop" or "sloop-of-war" might confuse a modern yachtsman. These vessels were, actually, small warships, light and comparatively fast, but with thin walls, flushdecked, carrying only one tier of guns. A sloop-of-war might be ship-rigged, or it might be brig-rigged, or schooner-rigged: it was never sloop-rigged.

16. History knows nothing more about this man. Not even his first name.

17. "This reads almost like target practice," is the comment of Hollis (*The Frigate Constitution,* p. 183). "In less than an hour he had cut off every stick of timber in the ship excepting part of the mainmast. Few of the *Java's* guns could be handled on account of the wreckage."

18. There probably never were more than 25,000 men under arms at any one time in the War of 1812, on the U.S. side, militia and regulars put together; and this out of a total population of more than $7\frac{1}{2}$ millions. Henry Adams has calculated that in proportion to population the Civil War effort was twenty times as great. *History*, Vol. VII, pp. 385-6.

19. "Two-thirds of the [British] troops in Canada were in fact fed on beef provided by American contractors and drawn chiefly from Vermont and New York." Fortescue, *British Army*, Vol. X, pp. 125-26.

20. Maclay, *American Privateers,* p. 506. He estimates that of the 500-odd American privateers who put forth, at least 300 came back empty-handed—or not at all. See also Coggeshall, Mahan, Cutler, Chapelle, Roosevelt, James, Barnes, in *Sources*. But the best discussion of privateering in the War of 1812 remains, and no doubt will remain, that of Henry Adams: *History,* Vol. VII, chap. 13; also Vol. VIII, chap. 7.

21. Here, and elsewhere in the book, military forces are computed as they were then—that is, by rank and file, or more accurately by effectives, which did not include sick, did not include musicians, and did not include sutlers or contractors, wives or prostitutes, or any other form of camp follower—though all of these had to be taken into consideration in rationing, of course, as in transportation—and also did not include sergeants or commissioned officers, though they did include corporals. To get the actual number of fighting men capable of being put into the field, about 7 per cent—it varied—should be added to the "effectives" figure in order to account for officers and sergeants.

22. By a dismounted cannon, which cannon can be seen today before Macdonough Hall, Annapolis.

23. Martell, *Side Light,* American Historical Review XLIII, pp. 553-66.

24. "These ideas [the Federalists', in Boston] were as genuine, as ingrained, in the average New England conscience of 1814 as were, in the South of 1860, a very similar set of *idées fixes,* which caused that section to secede from the Union. In 1814, the particular grievances of New England, that we have seen developing for the last decade, were, first, the restrictive system of Jefferson, now renewed; second, the loss of political influence by the ready admission of foreigners to franchise and to office, by the admission of new states out of the Louisiana

Purchase, and by slave representation; third, and most serious of all, the war." Morison, *Otis*, Vol. II, p. 71.

25. "Neither William Hull, Alexander Smyth, Dearborn, Wilkinson, nor Winchester showed such incapacity as [Brigadier General William H.] Winder either to organize, fortify, fight, or escape. When he might have prepared defences, he acted as scout; when he might have fought, he still scouted; when he retreated, he retreated in the wrong direction; when he fought, he thought only of retreat; and whether scouting, retreating, or fighting, he never betrayed an idea." Adams, *History*, Vol. VIII, p. 153.

26. "It is probably today the most widely used single term in human speech." Evans, *A Dictionary of Contemporary American Usage* (Random House, 1957). If etymologists, fascinated by this succinct and seemingly meaningless remark, have failed to come up with a satisfactory explanation of it, this is not because of lack of effort. The thing challenges. Scores of theories about O.K., all far-fetched, have been advanced. For instance, O.K. has been said to stand for *omnis korrecta,* a phrase once used by schoolmasters for marking examination papers; for rum from Aux Cayes in the West Indies, a notably reliable drink in its day; for Old Kinderhook, Martin Van Buren's summer home; for Obadiah Kelly, a freight-car checker who use to chalk his initials on railroad cars that were ready to go, etc., etc. We shall probably never know the truth. See *Dictionary of American English,* Vol. III, p. 1630; H. L. Mencken, *The American Language* (4th edition), pp. 205-08; W. S. Wyman in *Magazine of American History,* Vol. XIV, p. 212, who first pointed out that "oke" in Choctaw, a language with which Jackson must have been tolerably familiar, means "it is"; and, best of all, *"O.K."—But What do we Know About it?* by Woodford A. Heflin in *American Speech* of April, 1941, pp. 85-95, and William Bell Wait's article, *Richardson's "O.K." of 1815,* in the same issue.

27. A myth in his own lifetime, and much more of a myth after his death, Andrew Jackson was credited with saying many

things he probably never did say; but he might have *thought* that "the only good Indian is a dead Indian." This has been attributed to him. More often, however, it is attributed to William Tecumseh Sherman or to Philip Sheridan. See Bartlett, *Familiar Quotations* (1943 edition: Little, Brown) and Mencken, *New Dictionary of Quotations* (Knopf, 1942).

28. It was largely for her sake that the General, late in life, joined the Presbyterian Church. See Parton, Bassett, Eaton and Reid, Goodwin, Headley, Jenkins, Marquis James, Peterson, Johnson, Walker, Ward, Syrett, Sumner.

29. A modern military student might well be puzzled by these figures. Regiments in the early years of the nineteenth century were by no means as large as they are today. The U.S. Army did not have the almost inconceivably complicated regimental count that was practiced in the British Army, wherein the names of mythical persons were kept on the roster, openly, in order to bolster certain regimental funds; but the U.S. system was complicated enough. *Theoretically* an American regiment numbered about 600 rank and file. In fact, not one of them at this time was at full strength, and most—and this applies to all of the regiments under Jackson's command—had only about half strength or a little over, say, 350 effectives.

30. The General seemed to have a fondness for this word. "That banditti [Tecumseh's followers] ought to be swept from the face of the earth," he had written to William Henry Harrison from The Hermitage, November 28, 1811, and he had snorted when it was suggested that the United States might make use of Jean Lafitte's admittedly outside-the-law Baratarians, calling *them* "a hellish banditti."

31. George W. Erving of Massachusetts was commissioned plenipotentiary to Spain August 10.

32. *Writings,* Vol. II, p. 79.

33. *Correspondence,* II, 100.

34. The present Canal Street.

35. He is invariably called "commodore" in extemporaneous accounts; but the title was not official at that time, and when it came to be official it meant one rank above a captain, U.S.N., whereas "master-commander" at the time was, as the rank of "commander" is now, one rank *below* captain.

36. Bassett, *Life,* Vol. I, p. 157.

37. The site of the present Vicksburg.

38. From the diary of an unidentified British officer, found among the Jackson papers: "16th. Disembarked on a small Island, the whole of which except about 6 Acres was a compleat swamp, passed a cold night. 17th. Remained on the Island . . . a wet day, and the night colder than the last. 18th, 19th, and 20th. Remained on the Island. Suffered more from cold Since landing in this place than I did in all my Spbr [Spanish?] Campaigns. 21st. Embarked on board the Gun Vessels, where we remained all night." Bassett, Vol. II, p. 109.

39. That invaluable engineer, Major Latour, righteously indignant, gathered the names of as many of these fishermen as he could, and published these, "to consign them to execration and infamy." They are Maringuier, Old Luiz, Francisco, and Graviella, master fishermen, and Antonio el Italiano, El Campechano, Antonio El Portuguez, Manuelillo, Antonio El Mayorquin, and Garcia, hireling fishermen. *Historical Memoir,* pp. 82-83.

40. "The record of American generalship offered many examples of misfortune, but none so complete as this. Neither Hull nor Harrison, neither Winder nor Samuel Smith, had allowed a large British army, heralded long in advance, to arrive within seven miles unseen and unsuspected, and without so much as an earthwork, a man, or a gun between them and their object. The disaster was unprecedented, and could be repaired only by desperate measures." Adams, *History,* Vol. VIII, p. 339.

41. James, *Occurrences*, Vol. II, p. 355.

42. ". . . he was with good reason furious. To all intent his force was cooped on an isthmus three-quarters of a mile broad between the Mississippi and the swamp. In front was Jackson's fortified position; on the river were the enemy's armed vessels, flanking the only possible line of advance; and in the rear were the lake and the sea. The only base of supplies was some eighty miles distant, and accessible only in open boats; and the last four miles of this water-way were so narrow that it would hardly admit two boats abreast." Fortescue, Vol. X, p. 161. Fortescue, an Army man, blames Admiral Cochrane for this, though he cites no authority. We will never hear Packenham's own side of the story: he was killed in the battle.

43. Gleig, *Narrative,* p. 317.

44. "That Madison's authority could survive two such blows as the capture of Washington and the loss of Louisiana seemed improbable; but that he should resign was impossible, though the alternative was a collapse of government." Adams, *History,* Vol. VIII, p. 309.

45. July 14; but it was some weeks before the instruction reached the U.S. delegation in Europe, and some months before it was leaked to the British delegation.

46. "We are going to keep you young hot-heads from getting into mischief," the presiding officer, George Cabot, told a friend on the eve of his departure for the convention. Lodge, *Cabot,* p. 519. This was the day of the gunboat battle on Lake Borgne.

47. The rather startling equestrian statue of Jackson that stands in Lafayette Square, Washington, D.C.—it makes him look like a circus performer saluting the crowd—was cast in part from these guns, in part from some captured in the big battle.

48. The colonel was not there. The colonel seldom was, in the British Army of that time. Colonelcies could be highly remunerative, and they were bought and sold, or granted as royal favors, at Home. They had very little to do with warfare.

49. Jackson Square today.

50. His body was shipped back to England immersed in a barrel of rum, to preserve it.

51. *Authentic Narrative,* p. iii.

52. Appendix C.

Appendix A

Washington, June 1, 1812

To the Senate and House of Representatives of the United States:

I communicate to Congress certain documents, being a continuation of those heretofore laid before them on the subject of our affairs with Great Britain.

Without going back beyond the renewal in 1803 of the war in which Great Britain is engaged, and omitting unrepaired wrongs of inferior magnitude, the conduct of her Government presents a series of acts hostile to the United States as an independent and neutral nation.

British cruisers have been in the continued practice of violating the American flag on the great highway of nations, and of seizing and carrying off persons sailing under it, not in the exercise of a belligerent right founded on the law of nations against an enemy, but of a municipal prerogative over British subjects. British jurisdiction is thus extended to neutral vessels in a situation where no laws can operate but the laws of nations and the laws of the country to which the vessels belong, and a self-redress is assumed which, if British subjects were wrongfully detained and alone concerned, is that substitution of force for a resort to the responsible sovereign which falls within the definition of war. Could the seizure of British subjects in such cases be regarded as within the exercise of a belligerent right, the acknowledged laws of war, which forbid an article of captured property to be adjudged without a regular investigation before a competent tribunal, would imperiously demand the fairest

173

trial where the sacred rights of persons were at issue. In place of such a trial these rights are subjected to the will of every petty commander.

The practice, hence, is so far from affecting British subjects alone that, under the pretext of searching for these, thousands of American citizens, under the safeguard of public law and of their national flag, have been torn from their country and from everything dear to them; have been dragged on board ships of war of a foreign nation and exposed, under the severities of their discipline, to be exiled to the most distant and deadly climes, to risk their lives in the battles of their oppressors, and to be the melancholy instruments of taking away those of their own brethren.

Against this crying enormity, which Great Britain would be so prompt to avenge if committed against herself, the United States have in vain exhausted remonstrances and expostulations, and that no proof might be wanting of their conciliatory dispositions, and no pretext left for a continuance of the practice, the British Government was formally assured of the readiness of the United States to enter into arrangements such as could not be rejected if the recovery of British subjects were the real and the sole object. The communication passed without effect.

British cruisers have been in the practice also of violating the rights and the peace of our coasts. They hover over and harass our entering and departing commerce. To the most insulting pretensions they have added the most lawless proceedings in our very harbors, and have wantonly spilt American blood within the sanctuary of our territorial jurisdiction. The principles and rules enforced by that nation, when a neutral nation, against armed vessels of belligerents hovering near her coasts and disturbing her commerce are well known. When called on, nevertheless, by the United States to punish the greater offences committed by her own vessels, her Government has bestowed on their commanders additional marks of honor and confidence.

Under pretended blockades, without the presence of an adequate force and sometimes without the practicability of applying one, our commerce has been plundered in every sea, the great staples of our country have been cut off from their legitimate markets, and a destructive blow aimed at our agricultural and maritime interests. In aggravation of these predatory measures they have been considered as in force from the dates of their notification, a retrospective effect being thus added, as has been done in other important cases, to the unlawfulness of the course pursued. And to render the outrage the more signal these mock blockades have been reiterated and enforced in the face of official communications from the British Government declaring as the true definition of a legal blockade "that particular ports must be actually invested and previous warning given to vessels bound to them not to enter."

Not content with these occasional expedients to lay waste to our neutral trade, the cabinet of Britain resorted at length to the sweeping system of blockades, under the name of orders in council, which has been molded and managed as might best suit its political views, its commercial jealousies, or the avidity of British cruisers.

To our remonstrances against the complicated and transcendent injustice of this innovation the first reply was that the orders were reluctantly adopted by Great Britain as a necessary retaliation on decrees of her enemy proclaiming a general blockade of the British Isles at a time when the naval force of that enemy dared not issue from his own ports. She was reminded without effect that her own prior blockades, unsupported by an adequate naval force actually applied and continued, were a bar to this plea; that executed edicts against millions of our property could not be retaliation on edicts confessedly impossible to be executed; that retaliation, to be just, should fall on the party setting the guilty example, not on an innocent party which was not even chargeable with an acquiescence in it.

When deprived of this flimsy veil for a prohibition of our trade with her enemy by the repeal of his prohibition of our trade with Great Britain, her cabinet, instead of a corresponding repeal or a practical discontinuance of its orders, formally avowed a determination to persist in them against the United States until the markets of her enemy should be laid open to British products, thus asserting an obligation on a neutral power to require one belligerent to encourage by its internal regulations the trade of another belligerent, contradicting her own practice toward all nations, in peace as well as in war, and betraying the insincerity of those professions which inculcate a belief that, having resorted to her orders with regret, she was anxious to find an occasion for putting an end to them.

Abandoning still more all respect for the neutral rights of the United States and for its own consistency, the British Government now demands as prerequisites to a repeal of its orders as they relate to the United States that a formality should be observed in the repeal of the French decrees nowise necessary to their termination nor exemplified by British usage, and that the French repeal, besides including that portion of the decrees which operates within a territorial jurisdiction, as well as that which operates on the high seas, against the commerce of the United States should not be a single and special repeal in relation to the United States, but should be extended to whatever other neutral nations unconnected with them may be affected by those decrees. And as an additional insult, they are called on for a formal disavowal of conditions and pretensions advanced by the French Government for which the United States are so far from having made themselves responsible that, in official explanations which have been published to the world, and in a correspondence of the American minister at London with the British minister for foreign affairs such a responsibility was explicitly and emphatically disclaimed.

It has become, indeed, sufficiently certain that the commerce of the United States is to be sacrificed, not as interfering with the belligerent rights of Great Britain; not as supplying the wants of her enemies, which she herself supplies; but as interfering with the monopoly which she coverts for her own commerce and navigation. She carries on a war against the lawful commerce of a friend that she may the better carry on a commerce with an enemy—a commerce polluted by the forgeries and perjuries which are for the most part the only passports by which it can succeed.

Anxious to make every experiment short of the last resort of injured nations, the United States have withheld from Great Britain, under successive modifications, the benefits of a free intercourse with their market, the loss of which could not but outweigh the profits accruing from her restrictions of our commerce with other nations. And to entitle these experiments to the more favorable consideration they were so framed as to enable her to place her adversary under the exclusive operation of them. To these appeals her Government has been equally inflexible, as if willing to make sacrifices of every sort rather than yield to the claims of justice or renounce the errors of a false pride. Nay, so far were the attempts carried to overcome the attachment of the British cabinet to its unjust edicts that it received every encouragement within the competency of the executive branch of our Government to expect that a repeal of them would be followed by a war between the United States and France, unless the French edicts should also be repealed. Even this communication, although silencing forever the plea of a disposition in the United States to acquiesce in those edicts originally the sole plea for them, received no attention.

If no other proof existed of the predetermination of the British Government against a repeal of its orders, it might be found in the correspondence of the minister plenipotentiary of the United States at London and the British secretary for foreign affairs in 1810, on the question whether the blockade of May, 1806, was considered as in force or as not in force. It had been ascertained that the French Government, which urged this blockade as the ground of its Berlin decree, was willing in the event of its removal, to repeal that decree, which, being followed by alternate repeals of the other offensive edicts, might abolish the whole system on both sides. This inviting opportunity for accomplishing an object so important to the United States, and professed so often to be the desire of both the belligerents, was made known to the British Government. As that Government admits that an actual application of an adequate force is necessary to the existence of a legal blockade, and it was notorious that if such a force had ever been applied its long discontinuance had annulled the blockade in question, there could be no sufficient objection on the part of Great Britain to a formal revocation of it, and no imaginable objection to a declaration of the fact that the blockade did not exist. The declaration would have been consistent with her avowed principles of blockade, and would have enabled the United States to demand from France the pledged repeal of her decrees, either with success, in which case the way would have been opened for a general repeal of the belligerent edicts, or without success, in which case the United States would have been justified in turning their measures exclusively against France. The British Government would, however, neither rescind the Blackmail nor declare its nonexistence, nor permit its nonexistence to be inferred and affirmed by the American plenipotentiary. On the contrary, by representing the blockade to be comprehended in the orders in council, the United States were compelled so to regard it in their subsequent proceedings.

There was a period when a favorable change in the policy of the British cabinet was justly considered as established. The minister plenipotentiary of His Britannic Majesty here proposed an adjustment of the differences more immediately endangering the harmony of the two countries. The proposition was accepted with the promptitude and cordiality corresponding with the invariable professions of this Government. A foundation appeared to be laid for a sincere and lasting reconciliation. The prospect, however, quickly vanished. The whole proceeding was disavowed by the British Government without any explanations which could at that time repress the belief that the disavowal proceeded from a spirit of hostility to the commercial rights and prosperity of the United States; and it has since come into proof that at the very moment when the public minister was holding the language of friendship and inspiring confidence in the sincerity of the negotiation with which he was charged a secret agent of his Government was employed in intrigues having for their object a subversion of our Government and a dismemberment of our happy union.

In reviewing the conduct of Great Britain toward the United States our attention is necessarily drawn to the warfare just renewed by the savages on one of our extensive frontiers—a warfare which is known to spare neither age nor sex and to be distinguished by features peculiarly shocking to humanity. It is difficult to account for the activity and combinations which have for some time been developing themselves among tribes in constant intercourse with British traders and garrisons without connecting their hostility with that influence and without recollecting the authenticated examples of such interpositions heretofore furnished by the officers and agents of that Government.

Such is the spectacle of injuries and indignities which have been heaped on our country, and such the crisis which its unexampled forbearance and conciliatory efforts have not been able to avert. It might at least have been expected that an enlightened nation, if less urged by moral obligations or invited by friendly dispositions on the part of the United States, would have found its own interest alone a sufficient motive to respect their rights and their tranquillity on the high seas; that an enlarged policy would have favored that free and general circulation of commerce in which the British nation is at all times interested, and which in times of war is the best alleviation of its calamities to herself as well as to other belligerents; and more especially that the British cabinet would not, for the sake of a precarious and surreptitious intercourse with hostile markets, have persevered in a course of measures which necessarily put at hazard the invaluable market of a great and growing country, disposed to cultivate the mutual advantages of an active commerce.

Other counsels have prevailed. Our moderation and conciliation have had no other effect than to encourage perseverence and to enlarge pretensions. We behold our seafaring citizens still the daily victims of lawless violence, committed on the great common and highway of nations, even within sight of the country which owes them protection. We behold our vessels, freighted with the products of our soil and industry, or returning with the honest proceeds of them, wrested from their lawful destinations, confiscated by prize courts no longer the organs of public law but the instruments of arbitrary edicts, and their unfortunate crews dispersed and lost, or forced or inveigled in British ports into British fleets, whilst arguments are employed in support of these aggressions which have no foundation but in a principle equally supporting a claim to regulate our external commerce in all cases whatsoever.

We behold, in fine, on the side of Great Britain, a state of war against the United States, and on the side of the United States a state of peace toward Great Britain.

Whether the United States shall continue passive under these progressive usurpations and these accumulating wrongs, or, opposing force to force in defense of their national rights, shall commit a just cause into the hands of the Almighty Disposer of Events, avoiding all connections which might entangle it in the contest or views of other powers, and preserving a constant readiness to concur in an honorable re-establishment of peace and friendship, is a solemn question which the Constitution wisely confides to the legislative department of the Government. In recommending it to their early deliberations I am happy in the assurance that the decision will be worthy of the enlightened and patriotic councils of a virtuous, a free, and a powerful nation.

Having presented this view of the relations of the United States with Great Britain and of the solemn alternative growing out of them, I proceed to remark that the communications last made to Congress on the subject of our relations with France will have shewn that since the revocation of her decrees, as they violated the neutral rights of the United States, her Government has authorized illegal captures by its privateers and public ships, and that other outrages have been practiced on our vessels and our citizens. It will have been seen also that no indemnity had been provided or satisfactorily pledged for the extensive spoliations committed under the violent and retrospective orders of the French Government against the property of our citizens seized within the jurisdiction of France. I abstain at this time from recommending to the consideration of Congress definitive measures with respect to that nation, in the expectation that the result of unclosed discussions between our minister plenipotentiary at Paris and the French Government will speedily enable Congress to decide with greater advantage on the course due to the rights, the interests, and the honor of our country.

Appendix B

PROCLAMATION

Whereas the Congress of the United States, by virtue of the constituted authority vested in them, have declared by their act bearing date the 18th day of the present month that war exists between the United Kingdom of Great Britain and Ireland and the dependencies thereof and the United States of America and their Territories:

Now, therefore, I, James Madison, President of the United States of America, do hereby proclaim the same to all whom it may concern; and I do especially enjoin on all persons holding offices, civil or military, under the authority of the United States that they be vigilant and zealous in discharging the duties respectively incident thereto; and I do moreover exhort all the good people of the United States, as they love their country, as they value the precious heritage derived from the virtue and valor of their fathers, as they feel the wrongs which have forced on them the last resort of injured nations, and as they consult the best means under the blessing of Divine Providence of abridging its calamities, that they exert themselves in preserving order, in promoting concord, in maintaining the authority and efficacy of the laws, and in supporting and invigorating all the measures which may be adopted by the constituted authorities for obtaining a speedy, a just, and an honorable peace.

In testimony, etc.

Done, etc., the 19th day of June, 1812, etc.

Appendix C

THE TREATY OF GHENT

His Britannic Majesty and the United States of America desirous of terminating the war which has unhappily subsisted between the two Countries, and of restoring upon principles of perfect reciprocity, Peace, Friendship, and good Understanding between them, have for that purpose appointed their respective Plenipotentiaries, that is to say, His Britannic Majesty on His part has appointed the Right Honourable James Lord Gambier, late Admiral of the White now Admiral of the Red Squadron of His Majesty's Fleet; Henry Goulburn Esquire, a Member of the Imperial Parliament and Under Secretary of State; and William Adams Esquire, Doctor of Civil Laws: And the President of the United States, by and with the advice and consent of the Senate thereof, has appointed John Quincy Adams, James A. Bayard, Henry Clay, Jonathan Russell, and Albert Gallatin, Citizens of the United States; who, after a reciprocal communication of their respective Full Powers, have agreed upon the following Articles.

Article the First

There shall be a firm and universal Peace between His Britannic Majesty and the United States, and between respective Countries, Territories, Cities, Towns, and People of every degree without exception of places or persons. All hostilities both by sea and land shall cease as soon as this Treaty shall have been ratified by both parties as hereinafter mentioned. All territory, places, and possessions whatsoever taken by either party from the other during the war, or which may be taken after the signing of this Treaty, excepting only the Islands

185

hereinafter mentioned, shall be restored without delay and without causing any destruction or carrying away any of the Artillery or other public property originally captured in the said forts or places, and which shall remain therein upon the Exchange of the Ratifications of this Treaty, or any Slaves or other private property; And all Archives, Records, Deeds, and Papers, either of a public nature or belonging to private persons, which in the course of the war may have fallen into the hands of the Officers of either party, shall be, as far as may be practicable, forthwith restored and delivered to the proper authorities and persons to whom they respectively belong. Such of the Islands in the Bay of Passamaquoddy as are claimed by both parties shall remain in the possession of the party in whose occupation they may be at the time of the Exchange of the Ratifications of this Treaty until the decision respecting the title to the said Islands shall have been made in conformity with the fourth Article of this Treaty. No disposition made by this Treaty as to such possession of the Islands and territories claimed by both parties shall in any manner whatever be construed to affect the right of either.

Article the Second

Immediately after the ratifications of this Treaty by both parties as hereinafter mentioned, orders shall be sent to the Armies, Squadrons, Officers, Subjects, and Citizens of the two Powers to cease from all hostilities: and to prevent all causes of complaint which might arise on account of the prizes which may be taken at sea after the said Ratifications of this Treaty, it is reciprocally agreed that all vessels and effects which may be taken after the space of twelve days from the said Ratifications upon all parts of the Coast of North America from Latitude of twenty three degrees North to the Latitude of fifty degrees North, and as far Eastward in the Atlantic Ocean as the thirty sixth degree of West Longitude from the Meridian of Greenwich, shall be restored on each side:—that the time shall be thirty days in all other parts of the Atlantic Ocean

North of the Equinoctial Line or Equator:—and the same time for the British and Irish Channels, for the Gulf of Mexico, and all parts of the West Indies:—forty days for the North Seas for the Baltic, and for all parts of the Mediterranean:—sixty days for the Atlantic Ocean South of the Equator as far as the Latitude of the Cape of Good Hope:—ninety days for every other part of the world South of the Equator, and one hundred and twenty days for all other parts of the world without exception.

Article the Third

All Prisoners of war taken on either side as well by land as by sea shall be restored as soon as practicable after the Ratifications of this Treaty as hereinafter mentioned on their paying the debts which they have contracted during their captivity. The two Contracting Parties respectively engage to discharge in specie the advances which may have been made by the other for the sustenance and maintenance of such prisoners.

Article the Fourth

Whereas it was stipulated by the second Article in the Treaty of Peace of one thousand seven hundred and eighty three between His Britannic Majesty and the United States of America that the boundary of the United States should comprehend "all Islands within twenty leagues of any part of the shores of the United States and lying between lines to be drawn due East from the points where the aforesaid boundaries between Nova Scotia on the one part and East Florida on the other shall respectively touch the Bay of Fundy and the Atlantic Ocean, excepting such Islands as now are or heretofore have been within the limits of Nova Scotia," and whereas the several Islands in the Bay of Passamaquoddy, which is part of the Bay of Fundy, and the Island of Grand Menan in the said Bay of Fundy, are claimed by the United States as being comprehended within their aforesaid boundaries, which said Islands are claimed as belonging to His Britannic Majesty as having been at the time and previous to the aforesaid Treaty of one thousand seven hundred and eighty three within the limits of the Province of Nova Scotia: In order therefore finally to decide upon these claims it is agreed that they shall be referred to two Commissioners to be appointed in the following manner: viz: One Commissioner shall be appointed by His Britannic Majesty and one by the President of the United States, by and with the advice and consent of the Senate thereof, and the said two Commissioners so appointed shall be sworn impartially to examine and decide upon the said claims according to such evidence as shall be laid before them on the part of His Britannic Majesty and of the United States respectively. The said Commissioners shall meet at St Andrews in the Province of New Brunswick, and shall have power to adjourn to such other place or places as they shall think fit. The said Commissioners shall by a declaration or report under their hands and seals decide to which of the two Contracting parties the several Islands aforesaid do respectively belong in conformity with the true intent of the said Treaty of Peace of one thousand seven hundred and eighty three. And if the said Commissioners shall agree in their decision both parties shall consider such decision as final and conclusive. It is further agreed that in the event of the two Commissioners differing upon all or any of the matters so referred to them, or in the event of both or either of the said Commissioners refusing or declining or wilfully omitting to act as such, they shall make jointly or separately a report or reports as well to the Government of His Britannic Majesty as to that of the United States, stating in detail the points on which they differ, and the grounds upon which their respective opinions have been formed, or the grounds upon which they or either of them have so refused, declined or omitted to act. And His Britannic Majesty and the Government of the United States hereby agree to refer the report or reports of the said Commissioners to some friendly Sovereign or State to be then named for that purpose, and who shall be requested to decide on the differences which may be stated in the said report or reports, or upon the report of one Commissioner together with the grounds upon which the other Commissioner shall have refused, declined or omitted to act as the case may be. And if the Commissioner so refusing, declining, or omitting to act, shall also wilfully omit to state the grounds upon which he has done in such manner that the said statement may be referred to such friendly Sovereign or State together with the report of such other Commissioner, then such Sovereign or State shall decide ex parte upon the said report alone. And His Britannic Majesty and the Government of the United States engage to consider the decision of such friendly Sovereign or State to be final and conclusive on all the matters so referred.

Article the Fifth

Whereas neither that point of the Highlands lying due North from the source of the River St Croix, and designated in the former Treaty of Peace between the two Powers as the North West Angle of Nova Scotia, nor the North Westernmost head of Connecticut River has yet been ascertained; and whereas that part of the boundary line between the Dominions of the two Powers which extends from the source of the River St Croix directly North to the abovementioned North West Angle of Nova Scotia, thence along the said Highlands which divide those Rivers that empty themselves into the River St Lawrence from those which fall into the Atlantic Ocean to the North Westernmost head of Connecticut River, thence down along the middle of that River to the forty fifth degree of North Latitude, thence by a line due West on said latitude until it strikes the River Iroquois or Cataraquy, has not yet been surveyed: it is agreed that for these several purposes two Commissioners shall be appointed, sworn, and authorized to act exactly in the manner directed with respect to those mentioned in the next preceding Article unless otherwise specified in the present Article. The said Commissioners shall meet in St Andrews in the Province of New Brunswick, and shall have power to adjourn to such other place or places as they shall think fit. The said Commissioners shall have power to ascertain and determine the points above mentioned in conformity with the provisions of the said Treaty of Peace of one thousand seven hundred and eighty three, and shall cause the boundary aforesaid from the source of the River St Croix to the River Iroquois or Cataraquy to be surveyed and marked according to the said provisions. The said Commissioners shall make a map of the said boundary, and annex to it a declaration under their hands and seals certifying it to be the true Map of the said boundary, and particularizing the latitude and longitude of the North West Angle of Nova Scotia, of the North Western-most head of Connecticut River, and of such other points of the said boundary as they may deem proper. And both parties agree to consider such map and declaration as finally and con-clusively fixing the said boundary. And in the event of the said two Commissioners differing, or both, or either of them refusing, declining, or wilfully omitting to act, such reports, declarations or statements shall be made by them or either of them, and such reference to a friendly Sovereign or State shall be made in all respects as in the latter part of the fourth Article is contained, and in as full a manner as the same was herein repeated.

Article the Sixth

Whereas by the former Treaty of Peace that portion of the boundary of the United States from the point where the forty fifth degree of North Latitude strikes the River Iroquois or Cataraquy to the Lake Superior was declared to be "along the middle of said River into Lake Ontario, through the middle of said Lake until it strikes the communication by water between that Lake and Lake Erie, thence along the middle of said communication into Lake Erie, through the middle of said Lake until it arrives at the water communication into the Lake Huron; thence through the middle of said Lake to the water communication between that Lake and Lake Superior;"

and whereas doubts have arisen what was the middle of the said River, Lakes, and water communications, and whether certain Islands lying in the same were within the Dominions of His Britannic Majesty or of the United States: In order therefore finally to decide these doubts, they should be referred to two Commissioners to be appointed, sworn, and authorized to act exactly in the manner directed with respect to those mentioned in the next preceding Article unless otherwise specified in this present Article. The said Commissioners shall meet in the first instance at Albany in the State of New York, and shall have power to adjourn to such other place or places as they shall think fit. The said Commissioners shall by a Report or Declaration under their hands and seals, designate the boundary through the said River, Lakes, and water communications, and decide to which of the two Contracting parties the several Islands lying within the said Rivers, Lakes, and water communications, do respectively belong in conformity with the true intent of the said Treaty of one thousand seven hundred and eighty three. And both parties agree to consider such designation and decision as final and conclusive. And in the event of the said two Commissioners differing or both or either of them refusing, declining or wilfully omitting to act, such reports, declarations, or statements shall be made by them or either of them. And such reference to a friendly Sovereign or State shall be made in all respects as in the latter part of the fourth Article is contained, and in as full a manner as if the same was herein repeated.

Article the Seventh

It is further agreed that the said two last mentioned Commissioners after they shall have executed the duties assigned to them in the preceding Article, shall be, and they are hereby, authorized upon their oaths impartially to fix and determine according to the true intent of the said Treaty of Peace of one thousand seven hundred and eighty three, that part of the boundary between the dominions of the two Powers, which extends from the water communication between Lake Huron and Lake Superior to the most North Western point of the Lake of the Woods;—to decide which of the two Parties the several Islands lying in the Lakes, water communications, and Rivers forming the said boundary do respectively belong in conformity with the true intent of the said Treaty of Peace of one thousand seven hundred and eighty three, and to cause such parts of the said boundary as require it to be surveyed and marked. The said Commissioners shall by a Report or declaration under their hands and seals, designate the boundary aforesaid, state their decision on the points thus referred to them, and particularize the Latitude and Longitude of the most North Western point of the Lake of the Woods, and of such other parts of the said boundary as they may deem proper. And both parties agree to consider such designation and decision as final and conclusive. And in the event of the said two Commissioners differing, or both or either of them refusing, declining, or wilfully omitting to act, such reports, declarations or statements shall be made by them or either of them, and such reference to a friendly Sovereign or State shall be made in all respects as in the latter part of the fourth Article is contained, and in as full a manner as if the same was herein repeated.

Article the Eighth

The several Boards of two Commissioners mentioned in the four preceding Articles shall respectively have power to appoint a Secretary, and to employ such Surveyors or other persons as they shall judge necessary. Duplicates of all their respective reports, declarations, statements, and decisions, and of their accounts, and of the Journal of their proceedings shall be delivered by them to the Agents of His Britainnic Majesty and to the Agents of the United States, who may be respectively appointed and authorized to manage the business on behalf of their respective Governments. The said Commissioners shall be respectively paid in such manner as shall be agreed between the two contracting parties, such agreement being to be settled at the time of the Exchange of the Ratifications of this Treaty. And all other expenses attending the said Commissions shall be defrayed equally by the two parties. And in the case of death, sickness, resignation, or necessary absence, the place of every such Commissioner respectively shall be supplied in the same manner as such Commissioner was first appointed; and the new Commissioner shall take the same oath or affirmation and do the same duties. It is further agreed between the two contracting parties that in case any of the Islands mentioned in any of the preceding Articles, which were in the possession of one of the parties prior to the commencement of the present war between the two Countries, should by the decision of any of the Boards of Commissioners aforesaid, or of the Sovereign or State so referred to, as in the four next preceding Articles contained, fall within the dominions of the other party, all grants of land made previous to the commencement of the war by the party having had such possession, shall be as valid as if such Island or Islands had by such decision or decisions been adjudged to be within the dominions of the party having had such possession.

Article the Ninth

The United States of America engage to put an end immediately after the Ratification of the present Treaty to hostilities with all the Tribes or Nations of Indians with whom they may be at war at the time of such Ratification, and forthwith to restore to such Tribes or Nations respectively all the possessions, rights, and privileges which they may have enjoyed or been entitled to in one thousand eight hundred and eleven previous to such hostilities. Provided always that such Tribes or Nations shall agree to desist from all hostilities against the United States of America, their Citizens, and Subjects upon the Ratification of the present Treaty being notified to such Tribes or Nations, and shall so desist accordingly. And His Britannic Majesty engages on his part to put an end immediately after the Ratification of the present Treaty to hostilities with all the Tribes or Nations of Indians with whom He may be at war at the time of such Ratification, and forthwith to restore to such Tribes or Nations respectively all the possessions, rights, and privileges, which they may have enjoyed or been entitled to in one thousand eight hundred and eleven previous to such hostilities. Provided always that such Tribes or Nations shall agree to desist from all hostilities against His Britannic Majesty and His Subjects upon the Ratification of the present Treaty being notified to such Tribes or Nations, and shall so desist accordingly.

Article the Tenth

Whereas the Traffic in Slaves is irreconcilable with the principles of humanity and Justice, and whereas both His Majesty and the United States are desirous of continuing their efforts to promote its entire abolition, it is hereby agreed that both contracting parties shall use their best endeavors to accomplish so desirable an object.

Article the Eleventh

This Treaty when the same shall have been ratified on both sides without alteration by either of the contracting parties, and the Ratifications mutually exchanged, shall be binding on both parties, and the Ratifications shall be exchanged at Washington in the space of four months from this day or sooner if practicable.

In faith whereof, We the respective Plenipotentiaries have signed this Treaty, and have thereunto affixed our Seals.

Done in triplicate at Ghent the twenty fourth day of December one thousand eight hundred and fourteen.

> Gambier
> Henry Goulburn
> William Adams
> John Quincy Adams
> J. A. Bayard
> H. Clay
> Jona Russell
> Albert Gallatin

(This was ratified by Great Britain, December 31, 1814, and by the United States Senate, February 17, 1815. On the latter day, in Washington, the ratifications were formally exchanged. The treaty was proclaimed the following day.)

Sources

ADAMS, CHARLES FRANCIS, see ADAMS, JOHN QUINCY.

ADAMS, HENRY, editor, *Documents Relating to New-England Federalism, 1800-1815;* Boston: Little, Brown, & Co., 1905.

ADAMS, HENRY, *History of the United States during the Administration of James Madison,* 2 volumes; New York: Albert and Charles Boni, 1930.

ADAMS, HENRY, *History of the United States during the Administration of Thomas Jefferson,* 2 volumes; New York: Albert and Charles Boni, 1930.

ADAMS, HENRY, *John Randolph;* Boston: Houghton Mifflin Co., 1898.

ADAMS, HENRY, *The Life of Albert Gallatin;* New York: Peter Smith, 1943.

ADAMS, JOHN QUINCY, *Memoirs,* edited by Charles Francis Adams, 12 volumes; Philadelphia: J. B. Lippincott Co., 1874-77.

ALEXANDER, DEALVA STANWOOD, *A Political History of the State of New York,* 3 volumes; New York: Henry Holt & Co., 1906-09.

ALLEN, H. C., *Great Britain and the United States: A History of Anglo-American Relations, 1783-1952;* New York: St. Martin's Press, 1955.

ANDERSON, D. R., *The Insurgents of 1811;* Annual Report of the American Historical Association, 1913, Vol. I, pp. 165-76.

ANDERSON, D. R., *William Branch Giles: a Study in the Politics of Virginia and the Nation from 1790 to 1830;* Menasha, Wisconsin, 1915.

ANONYMOUS, *Civil and Military History of Andrew Jackson, by an American Officer;* New York: P. M. Davis, 1825.

ANONYMOUS, *Documents accompanying the Message of the President of the United States to the Two Houses of Congress at the Opening of the First Session of the Twelfth Congress;* Washington: R. C. Weightman, 1811.

ANONYMOUS, *Sketches of the War, between the United States and the British Isles;* Rutland, Vt.: Fay and Davison, 1815.

ARMSTRONG, JOHN, *Notices of the War of 1812,* 2 volumes; New York: George Dearborn, Publishers, 1836.

ARTHUR, STANLEY CLISBY, *Jean Lafitte, Gentleman Rover;* New Orleans: Harmonson, Publishers.

BABCOCK, KENRIC CHARLES, *The Rise of American Nationality, 1811-1819;* New York: Harper & Brothers, 1906.

BANCROFT, GEORGE, *History of the United States of America,* 6 volumes; New York: D. Appleton & Co., 1883.

BARNES, EDWARD, *History of the Late War between the United States and Great Britain,* 4 volumes; Philadelphia, 1823.

197

BARNES, HARRY ELMER, *The Second War for Independence;* American Mercury IV, 1925, pp. 469-75.

BARNES, JAMES, *Naval Actions of the War of 1812;* New York: Harper & Brothers, 1896.

BARTLETT, RUHL J., editor, *The Record of American Diplomacy: Documents and Readings in the History of American Foreign Relations;* New York: Alfred A. Knopf, Inc., 1948.

BASSETT, JOHN SPENCER, *The Life of Andrew Jackson,* 2 volumes; New York: Doubleday, Page & Co., 1911.

BASSETT, JOHN SPENCER, see JACKSON, ANDREW.

BASSETT, JOHN SPENCER, see TATUM, MAJOR HOWELL.

BEIRNE, FRANCIS F., *The War of 1812;* New York: E. P. Dutton & Co., Inc., 1949.

BEMIS, SAMUEL FLAGG, *A Diplomatic History of the United States;* New York: Henry Holt & Co., 1936.

BENTON, THOMAS HART, *Thirty Years' View,* 2 volumes; New York: D. Appleton & Co., 1854.

BEVERIDGE, ALBERT J., *The Life of John Marshall,* 2 volumes; Boston: Houghton Mifflin Co., 1929.

BOOKS, GEORGE S., see DURAND, JAMES.

BOYD, JOHN PARKER, *Documents and Facts relative to Military Events during the Late War;* 1816.

BOYD, JULIAN P., see JEFFERSON, THOMAS.

BRYANT, IRVING, *James Madison,* 5 volumes; Indianapolis: Bobbs-Merrill Co., 1941-56.

BRECKENRIDGE, HENRY M., *History of the Late War between the United States and Great Britain;* Baltimore: Joseph Gushing, 1817.

BROWN, CHARLES RAYMOND, *The Northern Confederacy, According to the Plans of the "Essex Junto," 1769-1814;* Princeton, N.J.: Princeton University Press, 1915.

BUELL, AUGUSTUS C., *History of Andrew Jackson: Pioneer, Patriot, Soldier, Politician, President,* 2 volumes; New York: Charles Scribner's Sons, 1904.

BURT, A. I., *The United States, Great Britain and British North America from the Revolution to the Establishment of Peace after the War of 1812;* New Haven: Yale University Press, 1940.

CADY, JOHN F., *Western Opinion and the War of 1812;* Ohio Archaeological and Historical Quarterly, XXXIII, 1924, pp. 427-76.

CARR, ALBERT Z., *The Coming of the War;* New York: Doubleday & Co., Inc., 1960.

CHADWICK, E. E., *The American Navy;* Brooklyn, 1828.

CHANNING, EDWARD, *A History of the United States,* 6 volumes; New York: The Macmillan Company, 1926.

CHANNING, EDWARD, *The Jeffersonian System, 1801-1811;* New York: Harper & Brothers, 1906.

CHAPELLE, HOWARD I., *American Sailing Craft;* New York: Kennedy Brothers, 1936.

CHAPELLE, HOWARD I., *The Baltimore Clipper: Its Origin and Development;* Salem, Mass.: The Marine Research Society, 1930.

CHAPELLE, HOWARD I., *The History of American Sailing Ships;* New York: W. W. Norton & Co., 1935.

COGGESHALL, GEORGE, *History of the American Privateers and Letters-of-Marque, during our War with England in the Years 1812, '13 and '14;* New York: published by and for the author, 1856.

COIT, MARGARET L., *John C. Calhoun: American Portrait;* Boston: Houghton Mifflin Co., 1950.

COLEMAN, CHRISTOPHER S., *The Ohio Valley in the Preliminaries of the War of 1812;* Mississippi Valley Historical Review, VII, pp. 39-50.

COLYAR, A. S., *Life and Times of Andrew Jackson: Soldier, Statesman, President,* 2 volumes; Nashville, Tenn.: Marshall & Bruce Company, 1904.

CRANE, STEPHEN, *Great Battles of the World;* London: Chapman & Hall, Ltd., 1901.

CULLUM, GEORGE W., *Campaigns of the War of 1812;* New York: J. Miller, 1879.

CUTLER, CARL, *Greyhounds of the Sea: the Story of the American Clipper Ship;* New York: Halcyon House, 1930.

DANGERFIELD, GEORGE, *The Era of Good Feelings;* New York: Harcourt, Brace & Co., 1952.

DAVIS, MAJOR P. M., *An Official and Full Detail of the Great Battle of New Orleans;* New York, 1836.

DAVIS, RICH DEWEY, *Financial History of the United States;* New York: Longmans, Green & Co., 1925.

DAWSON, HENRY BARTON, *Battles of the United States by Sea and Land,* 2 volumes; New York: Johnson, Fry & Co., 1858.

DURAND, JAMES, *James Durand, an Able Seaman of 1812: His Adventures on "Old Ironsides" and as an Impressed Sailor in the British Navy,* edited by George S. Books; New Haven: Yale University Press, 1926.

DWIGHT, THEODORE, *History of the Hartford Convention;* New York: N. & J. White; Boston: Russell, Odiorne & Co., 1833.

EATON, JOHN HENRY, and REID, JOHN, *The Life of Andrew Jackson;* Philadelphia: M. Carey & Son, 1817.

ELLIOTT, CHARLES BURKE, *The Doctrine of Continuous Voyage;* American Journal of International Law, Vol. I, Part I, pp. 61-104.

ELLIOTT, CHARLES WINSLOW, *Winfield Scott: the Soldier and the Man;* New York: The Macmillan Company, 1957.

EMMONS, G. F., *The Navy of the United States, 1775-1853;* Washington: 1853.

ESARY, LOGAN, see HARRISON, WILLIAM HENRY.

ESPOSITO, COL. VINCENT J., editor, *The West Point Atlas of American Wars,* 2 volumes; New York: Frederick A. Praeger, 1959.

FAULKNER, HAROLD UNDERWOOD, *American Economic History;* New York: Harper & Brothers, 1931.

FORESTER, C. S., *The Age of Fighting Sail: The Story of the Naval War of 1812;* Garden City, N.Y.: Doubleday & Co., 1956.

FORESTER, C. S., see WETHERELL, JOHN.

FORTESCUE, J. W., *History of the British Army,* 10 volumes; New York: The Macmillan Company, 1899-1920.

FORTIER, ALCEE, *History of Louisiana;* New York: Goupil & Co., 1904.

FULLER, H. B., *The Purchase of Florida: Its History and Diplomacy;* Cleveland, 1906.

FULLER, J. F. C., *Decisive Battle of the U.S.A.;* New York: Thomas Yoseloff, 1942.

GALES, JOSEPH, *War Manifesto of 1812;* American Historical Review, XIII, p. 303.

GANOE, WILLIAM ADDLEMAN, *The History of the United States Army;* (rev. ed.) New York and London: D. Appleton-Century Co., 1943.

GARDINER, ASA BIRD, *The Uniforms of the American Army;* Magazine of American History I, No. 8, August 1877.

GAY, SIDNEY HOWARD, *James Madison;* Boston: Houghton Mifflin & Co., 1884.

GAYARRE, CHARLES, *History of Louisiana: the American Domination;* New York: William J. Widdleton, Publisher, 1866.

GILMAN, DANIEL C., *James Monroe;* Boston: Houghton Mifflin & Co., 1883.

GILPIN, ERIC R., *The War of 1812 in the Old Northwest;* East Lansing, Mich.: Michigan State University Press, 1958.

GLEIG, GEORGE ROBFRT, *A Narrative of the Campaigns of the British Arms at Washington and New Orleans, under Generals Ross, Packenham and Lambert, in the Years 1814 and 1815;* London: John Murray, 1821.

GOODMAN, WARREN H., *The Origins of the War of 1812: a Survey of Changing Interpretations;* Mississippi Valley Historical Review, vol. XXVIII, No. 2.

HACKER, LOUIS M., *Western Land Hunger and the War of 1812: a Conjecture;* Mississippi Valley Historical Review, X, March 1924, pp. 365-95.

HAMILTON, STANISLAUS MURRAY, see MONROE, JAMES.

HARRISON, WILLIAM HENRY, *Messages and Letters,* 2 volumes, edited by Logan Esary; Indianapolis: Indiana Historical Commission, 1922.

HATCHER, WILLIAM B., *Edward Livingston: Jeffersonian Republican and Jacksonian Democrat;* Baton Rouge, La.: Louisiana State University Press, 1940.

HEADLEY, JOEL TYLER, *The Lives of Winfield Scott and Andrew Jackson;* New York: Charles Scribner, 1852.

HEADLEY, JOEL TYLER, *The Second War with England,* 2 volumes; New York: Charles Scribner's Sons, 1853.

HILDRETH, RICHARD, *The History of the United States of America,* 3 volumes; New York: Harper & Brothers, 1851-52.

HOLLIS, IRA N., *The Frigate Constitution: the Central Figure of the Navy under Sail;* Boston: Houghton Mifflin Company, 1900.

HOWARD, JOHN TASKER, *Our American Music: Three Hundred Years of it;* New York: Thomas Y. Crowell Co., 1930.

HUNT, GAILLARD, see MADISON, JAMES.

HUNTER, THERESA, *The Saga of Jean Lafitte: from Pirate to Patriot and Back Again;* San Antonio, Texas: The Naylor Company, 1940.

HUTCHINSON, J. R., *The Press-Gang, Afloat and Ashore;* New York: E. P. Dutton & Co., Inc., 1914.

INGERSOLL, CHARLES J., *Historical Sketch of the Second War Between the United States and Great Britain*, 3 volumes; Philadelphia: Lea and Blanchard, 1845.

JACKSON, ANDREW, *The Correspondence of Andrew Jackson*, edited by John Spencer Bassett, 6 volumes; Washington: The Carnegie Institution of Washington, 1926-35.

JACOBS, JAMES RIPLEY, *Tarnished Warrior: Major-General James Wilkinson*; New York: The Macmillan Co., 1938.

JAMES, MARQUIS, *Andrew Jackson, the Border Captain*; New York: The Literary Guild, 1933.

JAMES, WILLIAM, *A Full and Correct Account of the Military Occurrences of the Late War Between Great Britain and the United States of America*, 2 volumes; London: Printed for the author, 1818.

JENKINS, JOHN S., *The Generals of the Last War with Great Britain*; Auburn, N.Y.: Derby, Miller & Co., 1849.

JENNINGS, WALTER WILSON, *The American Embargo, 1807-1809*; Iowa City: University of Iowa Press, 1921.

JOHNSON, GERALD W., *Andrew Jackson: an Epic in Homespun*; New York: Milton, Balch & Co., 1927.

JOHNSON, ROSSITER, *A History of the War of 1812-15 between the United States and Great Britain*; New York: Dodd, Mead & Co., 1882.

KEENLEYSIDE, HUGH L., *Canada and the United States*; New York: Alfred A. Knopf, Inc., 1929.

KING, C. R., *Life and Correspondence of Rufus King*, 6 volumes; New York, 1894-1900.

KING, GRACE, *New Orleans: the Place and the People*; New York: The Macmillan Company, 1896.

KNOX, D. W., *History of the U.S. Navy*; Putnam, N.Y., 1948.

KOCH, ADRIENNE, *Jefferson and Madison: the Great Collaboration*; New York: Alfred A. Knopf, Inc., 1950.

LAFITTE, JEAN, *The Journal of Jean Lafitte: the Privateer-Patriot's Own Story*; New York: The Vantage Press, 1958.

LATHROP, JOHN, *A Compendious History of the Late War*; Boston: J. W. Burditt, 1815.

LATOUR, MAJOR A. LACARRIERE, *Historical Memoir of the War in West Florida and Louisiana, in 1814-15*, translated from the French by H. P. Nugent; Philadelphia: John Conrad & Co., 1816.

LEWIS, HOWARD T., *A Re-analysis of the Causes of the War of 1812*; Americana VI, 1911, pp. 506-85.

LOSSING, BENSON J., *The Pictorial Field Book of the War of 1812*; New York: Harper & Brothers, 1868.

LUCAS, CHARLES P., *The Canadian War of 1812*; Oxford: The Clarendon Press, 1926.

LUCAS, ROBERT, *Journal of the War of 1812*; Des Moines: State Historical Society of Iowa.

MCAFEE, ROBERT B., *The History of the Late War in the Western Country*; Bowling Green, Ky.: Historical Publications Co., 1919.

MACLAY, EDGAR STANTON, *A History of American Privateers;* New York and London: D. Appleton and Co., 1924.

MACLAY, EDGAR STANTON, *The History of the Navy, from 1775 to 1894,* 3 volumes; New York: D. Appleton & Co., 1895.

MADISON, JAMES, *The Writings of James Madison,* edited by Gaillard Hunt, 11 volumes; New York: G. P. Putnam's Sons, 1900.

MAHAN, A. T., *Sea Power and its Relations to the War of 1812,* 2 volumes; Boston: Little, Brown & Co., 1919.

MARTELL, J. S., *A Side Light on Federalist Strategy;* American Historical Review, XLIII, pp. 553-66.

MALONE, DUMAS, *Jefferson, the Virginian;* Boston: Little, Brown & Co., 1948.

MARINE, WILLIAM M., *The British Invasion of Maryland, 1812-1815;* Baltimore: Society of the War of 1812 in Maryland, 1913.

MARTIN, FRANCOIS XAVIER, *History of Louisiana;* New Orleans: James A. Gresham, 1882.

MASEFIELD, JOHN, *Sea Life in Nelson's Time;* New York: The Macmillan Company, 1937.

MILLER, HUNTER, ed., *Treaties and Other International Acts of the United States of America,* 8 volumes; Washington: Government Printing Office, 1931.

MONROE, JAMES, *The Writings of James Monroe,* edited by Stanislaus Murray Hamilton, 8 volumes; New York: G. P. Putnam's Sons, 1898.

MONROE, JAMES, see GILMAN, DANIEL C.

MORISON, SAMUEL ELIOT, *Life and Letters of Harrison Gray Otis, 1765-1848,* 2 volumes; Boston: Houghton Mifflin Co., 1913.

MULLER, CHARLES G., *The Proudest Day;* New York: The John Day Company, 1960.

MYERS, GUSTAVUS, *The History of Tammany Hall;* New York: Boni & Liveright, 1917.

O'CONNOR, THOMAS, *An Impartial and Correct History of the War between the United States and Great Britain;* New York: John Low, 1815.

OGG, FREDERIC AUSTIN, *The Opening of the Mississippi: A Struggle for Supremacy in the American Interior;* New York: The Macmillan Company, 1904.

NICOLSON, HAROLD, *The Congress of Vienna: a Study in Allied Unity, 1812-1822;* New York: Harcourt, Brace & Co., 1946.

NUGENT, H. P., see LATOUR, MAJOR A. LaCARRIERE.

PAINE, RALPH D., *The Fight for a Free Sea: a Chronicle of the War of 1812;* New Haven: Yale University Press, 1920.

PARSONS, EDWARD ALEXANDER, *Jean Lafitte in the War of 1812: a Narrative Based on the Original Documents;* Worcester, Mass.: American Antiquarian Society, 1941.

PARTON, JAMES, *The Life of Andrew Jackson,* 3 volumes; New York: Mason Bros., 1860.

PATRICK, REMBERT W., *Florida Fiasco: Rampant Rebels on the Georgia-Florida Border, 1810-1815;* Athens, Ga.: University of Georgia Press, 1954.

PAXSON, FREDERIC L., *History of the American Frontier, 1763-1893;* Boston: Houghton Mifflin Co., 1924.

PERKINS, SAMUEL, *History of the Political and Military Events of the Late War;* New Haven, Conn.: 1854.

PETERSON, CHARLES J., *The Military Heroes of the War of 1812;* Philadelphia: Leary & Getz, 1854.

PICKERING, OCTAVUS, and UPHAM, CHARLES WENTWORTH, *The Life of Timothy Pickering,* 4 volumes; Boston: Little, Brown & Co., 1867-73.

POAGE, GEORGE RAWLINGS, *Henry Clay and the Whig Party;* Chapel Hill, N.C.: University of North Carolina Press, 1936.

PRATT, FLETCHER, *The Navy, a History;* Garden City, N.Y.: Doubleday, Doran & Co., 1938.

PRATT, JULIUS W., *Expansionists of 1812;* New York: The Macmillan Company, 1925.

REID, JOHN, see EATON, JOHN HENRY

ROOSEVELT, THEODORE, *Gouverneur Morris;* Boston: Houghton Mifflin & Co., 1891.

ROOSEVELT, THEODORE, *The Naval War of 1812;* New York: Charles Scribner's Sons, 1926.

ROWLAND, MRS. DUNBAR, *Andrew Jackson's Campaign against the British, or, The Mississippi Territory in the War of 1812;* New York: The Macmillan Company, 1926.

ROWLAND, KATE MASON, *The Life of Charles Carroll of Carrollton, 1737-1832,* 2 volumes; New York and London: G. P. Putnam's Sons, 1899.

RUSSELL, PHILLIPS, *Jefferson: Champion of the Free Mind;* New York: Dodd, Mead & Co., 1956.

SARGENT, EPES, *The Life and Public Services of Henry Clay;* New York: Greeley & McElrath, 1844.

SAXON, LYLE, *Fabulous New Orleans;* New York: The Century Company, 1928.

SAXON, LYLE, *Lafitte the Pirate;* New York: The Century Company, 1930.

SCHACHNER, NATHAN, *Thomas Jefferson: a Biography,* 2 volumes; New York: Appleton-Century-Crofts, Inc., 1951.

SCHLESINGER, ARTHUR M., JR., *The Age of Jackson;* Boston: Little, Brown & Co., 1945.

SCHURZ, CARL, *Life of Henry Clay,* 2 volumes; Boston: Houghton Mifflin Company, 1887.

SCOTT, WINFIELD, *Memoirs of Lieut.-General Scott, LL.D., written by Himself,* 2 volumes; New York: Sheldon & Company, 1864.

SINCLAIR, HAROLD, *The Port of New Orleans;* Garden City, N.Y.: Doubleday & Co., 1942.

SHREVE, R. O., *The Finished Scoundrel: General James Wilkinson;* Indianapolis: The Bobbs-Merrill Co., 1933.

SCHOULER, JAMES, *History of the United States of America under the Constitution,* 6 volumes; New York: Dodd, Mead & Co., 1882.

SMITH, THEODORE CLARK, *War Guilt in 1812;* Massachusetts Historical Society Proceedings LXIV, 1931, pp. 319-45.

SONNACK, OSCAR GEORGE THEODORE, *Report on "The Star-Spangled Banner," "Hail Columbia," "America," "Yankee Doodle";* Washington: Government Printing Office, 1909.

SONNACK, OSCAR GEORGE THEODORE, *"The Star-Spangled Banner";* Washington: Government Printing Office, 1914 (revised and enlarged from the *"Report"*).

SPEARS, JOHN R., *The American Slave-Trade: an Account of its Origin, Growth and Suppression;* New York: Charles Scribner's Sons, 1901.

STEELE, MATTHEW F., *American Campaigns,* 2 volumes; Washington: Byron S. Adams, 1909.

STEVENS, WILLIAM OLIVER, *Pistols at Ten Paces: the Story of the Code of Honor in America;* Boston: Houghton Mifflin Co., 1949.

STRAUS, RALPH, *Lloyd's: The Gentlemen at the Coffee-House;* New York: Carrick & Evans, Inc., 1938.

SUMNER, WILLIAM GRAHAM, *Andrew Jackson;* Boston: Houghton Mifflin Co., 1882.

SWANSON, NEIL H., *The Perilous Fight;* New York: Farrar & Rinehart, 1945.

SYRETT, HAROLD C., *Andrew Jackson, His Contribution to the American Tradition;* Indianapolis: The Bobbs-Merrill Co., Inc., 1953.

TATUM, HOWELL, *Major Howell Tatum's Journal, while Acting Topographical Engineer (1814) to General Jackson, Commanding the Seventh Military District,* edited by John Spencer Bassett; Northampton, Mass.: Smith College Studies in History, 1922.

THOMAS, DAVID YANCEY, *A History of Military Government in Newly Acquired Territory of the United States;* New York: Columbia University Press, 1904.

THOMSON, J. L., *Historical Sketches of the Late War;* Philadelphia, 1818.

THOMSON, J. L., *History of the War of the United States with Great Britain in 1812 and the War with Mexico;* Philadelphia, 1873.

TRUMBULL, JOHN, *Autobiography, Reminiscences and Letters, from 1756 to 1841;* New Haven, Conn.: B. L. Hamlen, 1841.

TUPPER, F. B., *Life and Correspondence of Major-General Sir Isaac Brock;* London, 1845.

UPDYKE, FRANK A., *The Diplomacy of the War of 1812;* Baltimore: The Johns Hopkins Press, 1915.

UPHAM, CHARLES WENTWORTH, see PICKERING, OCTAVIUS.

VAN TYNE, CHARLES H., *Why Did We Fight in 1812? The Causes and Significance of Our Last War with Great Britain;* Independent, LXXIV, 1913, pp. 1327-1331.

VERRILL, A. HYATT, *Smugglers and Smuggling;* New York: Duffield & Co., 1924.

VON HOLST, DR. H., *John C. Calhoun;* Boston: Houghton Mifflin & Co., 1882.

WALKER, ALEXANDER, *The Life of Andrew Jackson, to which is added an Authentic Narrative of the Memorable Achievements of the American*

Army at New Orleans, in the Winter of 1814, '15; Philadelphia: G. G. Evans, Publisher, 1860.

WALTERS, RAYMOND, JR., *Albert Gallatin, Jeffersonian Financier and Diplomat;* New York: The Macmillan Company, 1957.

WARD, JOHN WILLIAM, *Andrew Jackson, Symbol for an Age;* New York: Oxford University Press, 1955.

WECTER, DIXON, *The Hero in America: a Chronicle of Hero-Worship;* New York: Charles Scribner's Sons, 1941.

WEINBERG, ALBERT K., *Manifest Destiny: a Study of Nationalist Expansionism in American History;* Baltimore: Johns Hopkins Press, 1935.

WERNER, M. R., *Tammany Hall;* New York: Doubleday, Doran & Co., 1928.

WILKINSON, JAMES, *Memoirs of My Own Times,* 3 volumes; Philadelphia: Abraham Small, 1816.

WOOD, WILLIAM, *The War with the United States, a Chronicle of 1812;* Toronto: Glasgow, Brook & Company, 1920.

ZIMMERMAN, JAMES FULTON, *Impressment of American Seamen;* New York: Columbia University Press, 1925.

Index

207